Holy Spirit

Other books in the Lutheran Voices series

LUTHERAN VOICES

Holy Spirit
Creative Power in Our Lives

Lois Malcolm

Augsburg Fortress

Minneapolis

HOLY SPIRIT
Creative Power in Our Lives

Purchases of multiple copies of this book are available at a discount from the publisher. For more information, contact the sales department at Augsburg Fortress, Publishers, 1-800-328-4648, or write to: Sales Director, Augsburg Fortress, Publishers, Box 1209, Minneapolis, MN 55440-1209.

Materials for a single- or multiple-session study of *Holy Spirit* are downloadable free of charge at www.augsburgfortress.org.

Scripture quotations, unless otherwise marked, are from the New Revised Standard Version Bible, copyright © 1989 by the Division of Christian Education of the National Council of Churches of Christ in the USA. Used by permission. All rights reserved.

Cover image © iStockphoto.com/Christine Glade.

Library of Congress Cataloging-in-Publication Data

Malcolm, Lois, 1959-
  Holy Spirit : creative power in our lives / Lois Malcolm.
     p. cm. — (Lutheran voices series)
  Includes bibliographical references and index.
  ISBN 978-0-8066-7058-4 (alk. paper)
  1. Holy Spirit. 2. Christian life. I. Title.
BT123.M35 2009
231'.3—dc22

                              2009021839

The paper used in this publication meets the minimum requirements of American National Standard for Information Sciences—Permanence of Paper for Printed Library Materials, ANSI Z329.48-1984. Manufactured in the U.S.A.

Manufactured in the U.S.A.

Contents

Acknowledgments

I am especially grateful to my editor, Susan Johnson, who has insightfully guided the writing of this book from the very beginning. She is truly the midwife of this book. I am also grateful to Victoria Smith for helpful comments on drafts of the book's chapters and to Andrew Nelson for proofreading.

I am very grateful to the many students who have taken my Holy Spirit course at Luther Seminary over the years. Their provocative questions about the Holy Spirit have informed almost every page of this book. My only hope is that I have done justice to the honesty and intensity of their questions and insights.

I am grateful to the friends and colleagues who encouraged and supported me while I was writing this book, especially David Watkins and Janet Ramsey.

Finally, I am most grateful to my parents, Robert Calvin Malcolm and Kari Marie Torjesen Malcolm for embodying the Spirit's presence in every aspect of their lives. Even now, although my mother has Alzheimer's—and can no longer articulate a coherent sentence—she radiates a joy, a peace, and a profound love for all she encounters that can only be described as the "fruit" of the Spirit. And, my father's passionate loyalty and care for her, in spite of his deep grief over what is happening to her, is a palpable testimony of the Spirit's power to work even in the most difficult of circumstances. Her radiant eyes and his youthful energy embody nothing other than the Spirit's creative life and power.

Introduction

Every year, when I teach the Holy Spirit course for seniors at Luther Seminary, I begin by asking these two questions: Who is the Holy Spirit? Have you experienced the Spirit in your life and in the world around you? As my students try to respond, they often draw a blank. Many of them tell me that this is the first time someone has asked them directly about the Holy Spirit's presence and activity in their lives. "We have never really thought much about the Holy Spirit," they say, "and as for experiences of the Spirit, do normal people actually have them?"

Like my students, many of us are at a loss for words when it comes to talk about the Holy Spirit. We leave experiences of the Spirit to *other* people—enthusiasts, charismatics, and mystics. We may say we believe in God, but for the most part, we think, act, and feel as though God's Spirit were not really a part of our lives.

Even our churches do not give us much guidance on the Holy Spirit. They plod along—with their plans and internal conflicts—as though they were solely human institutions without any real sense of God's vitality and presence. No wonder we turn elsewhere when we hit a crisis in our lives, such as depression or divorce or having to deal with an addiction. We turn to self-help books or to spiritual teachers from other religious traditions or to support groups outside of the church for help with spirituality and a sense of how God—or a higher power—might actually transform our lives. No wonder many people who were raised in church have now left the church, seeking meaning and purpose for their lives elsewhere.

Yet the Bible is full of stories about the Spirit's life and creative power. As we open ourselves up to what these stories have to say about the Spirit, we experience the energizing force—the vitality—that transforms us. We discover that the Spirit imbues every moment of our lives with God's inexhaustible life. We discover that every moment can be lived with the newness and freshness of that life. We discover gifts we never thought we had. We discover a fierce desire for truth—a hunger for justice and righteousness—that affects all our relationships and activities. We no longer are able to look at ourselves or other people in the same way.

Through the Spirit, we are transformed, regardless of who we are or what our circumstances in life might be. We discover that faith is about living with a freedom, a joy, and a peace that the circumstances in our life cannot affect. We discover a love that enables us to be more fully ourselves and thus able to love the people in our lives more fully and more deeply. We discover a hope that inspires even when we experience what would otherwise defeat us.

My hope is that as you read this little book, you will have a taste of the Spirit creating faith, love, and hope within you, and that you will be able to share that taste with others. I urge you to keep a journal while you read each chapter. More important than the content of this book is your own bold encounter with the Spirit's creative power and life. I pray that as you read this book, you will, through the Spirit, be more deeply grounded in your identity in Christ and in the full breadth, depth, and height of God's love for you and for all people (Eph. 3:14-19).

1

The Spirit of God in the Old Testament

Why stress the importance of the Old Testament at the beginning of a book on spiritual experience? Because the Old Testament reminds us that the experience of the Spirit is never merely an inward experience of God's presence nor merely a charismatic experience of extraordinary power—although it includes these things!

Early on in the second century, Christians rejected "Gnostic" spirituality, the kind of spirituality that links salvation with the individual soul's being freed from the body and all its vulnerable frailty. If there is anything about the good news Jesus brings to our lives, it is that salvation has to do with the resurrection of our bodies. The Spirit raised Jesus' body from the dead and will be "pour[ed] out on all flesh" in order to make it alive eternally (Joel 2:28). Our bodies are the temple of the Holy Spirit. "The body is meant . . . for the Lord, and the Lord for the body" (1 Cor. 6:13). The Spirit is present among us as the body of Christ (1 Cor. 12).

In rejecting Gnosticism, early Christians realized that they needed to include the Old Testament as part of their Scripture. Why? Because it reminds us that the Spirit who raised Jesus from the dead and who lives within and among us as Christ's Spirit, is always the same Spirit who creates and continues to create—by breathing life into all created bodies, into all human beings, and into all of creation itself. Moreover, the Old Testament reminds us that the Spirit within our personal lives, and the Spirit who gives us as individuals charismatic power to do extraordinary things at certain times, is also always a Spirit who works within our societies, bringing about justice and peace, especially for those who have the least power. Most importantly, the Old Testament reminds us that everything Christians have to say about the power of Jesus' resurrection and the power of the Spirit among us only has significance against the backdrop of God's promise to Israel. What is that promise? It is the promise of a time when the Messiah will usher in a new age when God's Spirit will be poured out not only on all people but also on the entire natural world—empowering all creatures to live in the peace and harmony of God's reign that imbues all of life.

The Meaning of "Spirit" in the Old Testament

To understand what the Old Testament means by "spirit," we have to forget our everyday use of the word. We often use "spirit" to mean something different from the body and matter—to mean something we experience beyond the senses. By contrast, the Old Testament uses "spirit" (*ruach*) to mean something that *lives* in contrast to what is dead. You know you are alive when you inhale and exhale air. The Hebrew word for spirit (*ruach*) refers to the "breath of life" and the "power that gives life." God's *ruach* gives us the breath to live—to be a human *ruach* in our own right. God breathed life into the first human being, turning him from dust into a human being (Gen. 2:7). When God takes away our breath, we die and return to dust. When God sends forth God's Spirit, we are created and the "face of the ground" is renewed (Ps. 104:29-30; see also Job 33:4). God preserves our spirits with care, life, and steadfast love (Job 10:12), even amidst experiences of anguish when God's face seems to be hidden from us (Job 7:11).

As the very breath of our life, God's Spirit confronts us with God's personal presence—both within us and throughout the entire universe. The psalmist cries out,

Where can I go from your [*ruach*]?
    Or where can I flee from your presence?
If I ascend to heaven, you are there;
    if I make my bed in Sheol, you are there.
If I take the wings of the morning
    and settle at the farthest limits of the sea,
even there your hand shall lead me,
    and your right hand shall hold me fast. (Ps. 139:7-10)

Probably an onomatopoetic word for a gale—like the strong east wind that divided the Red Sea when the Hebrew slaves fled Egypt (Exod. 14:21)—*ruach* also describes the palpable way people experience the irresistible force of the Creator's power. At crucial points in Israel's history, God appears as wind and as fire: as the "I am" that appears to Moses in the burning bush in Exodus 3 or as the thunder and lightning that accompanies the giving of the Ten Commandments on the mountain of Sinai in Exodus 19-20. The prophets describe God's killing wrath and life-giving mercy with images of a "stormy wind" (Ezek. 13:13) and the "spirit of burning" that washes away filth and cleanses bloodstains (Isa. 4:4).

In addition, the word *ruach* is probably related to *rewah*, meaning "breadth." *Ruach* creates space. It sets in motion. It leads out of narrow places into wide vistas, thus conferring life. The psalmist declares, "Out of my distress, I called on the Lord; the Lord answered me and set me in a broad place" (Ps. 118:5; see also Ps. 18:19 and 31:8). In the midst of our affliction and adversities, God brings us to a "spacious place," a space where life can unfold freely, without restriction (Ps. 66:12; see also Gen. 26:22).

The Charismatic Spirit of Judges and Kings

Scripture records how the God of Israel acted in history. God appeared to Abraham, promising him land and descendants, in spite of his wife's old age and barren womb (Genesis 18). God appeared to Moses in the burning bush, giving him the power to lead Abraham's descendants out of their oppression and affliction as slaves in Egypt (Exod. 3). Then, as they began to establish themselves as a nation, the Spirit of God acted through judges who were given extraordinary power—*charismatic power*—to lead Israel in defeating their enemies. Moses laid his hands on Joshua so that, filled with the "spirit of wisdom," he could lead the people of Israel into the Promised Land (Deut. 34:9). The Spirit came upon Othniel (Judg. 3:10), the prophetess Deborah (Judg. 4), and Jephthah (Judg. 11:29). More familiar to us are the stories of the Spirit coming on Gideon, who demonstrated that God could work through a small "remnant" (Judg. 6:34; 7:2), and Samson, who performed legendary feats as long as he did not cut his hair (Judg. 13:25; 14:6-9; 15:15).

The extraordinary power these individuals received was temporary; they received power to perform a specific task for the people. And, although prayers for God's help often preceded the coming of the Spirit (3:10; 4:3; 16:28), these experiences of ecstatic power were not yet distinctively Israelite. The stories are similar to many other stories from the ancient world—a world full of good and evil spirits influencing human affairs, and a world full of prophets, seers, and charismatic leaders inspired with spiritual power. When the people of Israel began to yearn for a king, the prophet Samuel (a former seer), poured oil on Saul's head and the Spirit of God put Saul into a prophetic frenzy that turned him into a different person, a person ready to be king (1 Sam. 10:1, 6). But when Saul failed as king, Samuel anointed David and the Spirit departed from Saul, coming "mightily" instead on David and remaining on him "from that day forward" (1 Sam. 16:13). Later, Nathan (another prophet) declared to David that God would establish his kingdom forever and that God's mercy would remain with him. God would be his father and he would be God's son (2 Sam. 7:14), a theme echoed in the Psalms: "You are my son; today I have begotten you" (Ps. 2:7).

Anointed by God's Spirit, the kings embodied God's special relationship to the people of Israel, also called God's "firstborn son" (Exod. 4:22). This special relationship with God, akin to that of a beloved child to a parent, was a relationship defined by God's steadfast love and God's expectation that the people live righteous lives governed by God's justice and mercy. As we will see, expectations for a Messiah drew heavily on this image of a king anointed by the Spirit to embody God's special relationship with God's people.

The Ethical Spirit of the Prophets

Prophets guided kings at critical points in Israel's history. They had insight into God's will at crucial junctures, and reminded people that God's power was always an ethical power that upheld God's justice and righteousness. Nathan, for example, confronted David with his sin of adultery and murder, reminding him that his power depends on God's just and righteous power, something that was quite revolutionary for a time when people thought kings had absolute power (see 2 Sam. 11:1–12:23).

True prophets, like Elijah and Obadiah in the time of king Ahab, spoke the truth about a situation, even if it meant bad news (see 1 Kings 18:12). False prophets merely told the king what he wanted to hear. Of course, prophets sometimes disagreed—thus, the crucial need to discern the spirits for whom the prophets spoke. Just because they had ecstatic charismatic experiences did not necessarily mean that their insight into a situation was true insight (see 1 Kings 22:24-28).

The later "classical," pre-exilic prophets—Amos, Hosea, Micah, Isaiah, and Jeremiah—tended not to draw their authority to speak from the "Spirit of God." Rather, they drew their authority from "God's word" (*dabar*), prefacing what they had to say with: "Thus says the Lord...." Speaking the "word of the Lord," they spoke out against the injustice of political and religious leaders who exploited the poor and powerless. They were especially critical of people who performed religious practices while oppressing and exploiting the poor, and they frequently criticized false prophets who merely said what those in power wanted them to say.

Amos, a herdsman, spoke out against social injustice—the way people trampled on the poor and needy and sold debtors into slavery—and warned of God's impending judgment (Amos 2:6-7). Hosea used prostitution and adultery as metaphors to describe how Israel abandoned her relationship with God by worshiping the old gods of the land and seeking foreign alliances. Although he relied on "the word of the Lord" (Hos. 1:1) for his authority, he did speak of the prophet as a "man of spirit" (Hos. 9:7) and spoke of a "wind" of judgment (Hos. 4:19). With Micah, we have the first instance of a prophet explicitly linking the Spirit's power—and not merely God's word—with a call for justice (Mic. 3:8). He spoke out against the way corrupt religious and political leaders exploited the poor and powerless and warned of God's coming judgment, calling for people to "do justice, and to love kindness, and to walk humbly with your God" (Mic. 6:8).

Jeremiah railed against how "everyone is greedy for unjust gain . . . from prophet to priest"—treating the "wound of my people carelessly, saying, 'Peace, peace,' when there is no peace'" (Jer. 6:13-14). At the heart of his jeremiads was the constant refrain that God's "steadfast love, justice, and righteousness" were the only causes for "boasting"—not human wisdom, might, or wealth (Jer. 9:23-24). Yet in spite of his frustration with the people's injustice, Jeremiah delivered God's promise to make a new covenant with God's people: "I will put my law within them, and I will write it on their hearts; and I will be their God and they shall be my people. No longer shall they teach one another, or say to each other, 'Know the Lord,' for they shall all know me, from the least of them to the greatest . . . for I will forgive their iniquity, and remember their sins no more" (Jer. 31:33-4).

The Spirit of Messianic Hope

As the people of Israel faced the decline of their national stability and as they experienced exile as prisoners of war in Babylon (587 BCE), there emerged among them an expectation for the coming "day of the Lord." On that day, the Spirit would come as *judgment*— a burning that washes away the "filth" and "bloodstains" of unrighteousness and injustice (Isa. 4:4)—and as *promise*—as the Spirit and blessing God promises to pour on their descendants (Isa. 44:3).

On the "day of the Lord," a savior-king would come, a Messiah from the line of David, to bring rebirth to a dying Israel. The Spirit would rest upon this king, giving him "the spirit of wisdom and understanding, the spirit of counsel and might, the spirit of knowledge and the fear of the Lord" (Isa. 11:2). This king would bring righteousness and justice to the poor and "meek of the earth," and judge their oppressors harshly (11:3-5).

Along with this expectation of a savior-king, there also emerged the hope for a Servant who, through the Spirit's power, would "bring forth justice to the nations" and not "grow faint or be crushed until he has established justice in the earth" (Isa. 42:1, 4). This Servant was also seen as a Suffering Servant, who, as one who was righteous, made many others righteous and whole, not only by bearing their infirmities and diseases, but also by being afflicted by God for their sins: "But he was wounded for our transgressions, crushed for our iniquities; upon him was the punishment that made us whole, and by his bruises we are healed" (Isa. 53:5).

In the oracles written after the return from exile in 539 BCE, this image of a Servant was echoed in the portrayal of a prophet anointed by the Spirit of God, whose task was: "to bring good news to the oppressed, to bind up the brokenhearted, to proclaim liberty to the captives, and release to the prisoners; to proclaim the year of the Lord's favor, and the day of vengeance of our God; to comfort all who mourn. . . ." (Isa. 61:1-2; see also Luke 4:18-21).

What would characterize the reign of this Messiah? It would be a reign of peace and harmony not only among people, but also within the natural world. Isaiah painted a graphic picture of wolves living with lambs, leopards lying down with kids, cows grazing with bears, and little children playing with snakes. Indeed, a "little child" would lead "the calf and the lion and fatling together" and nothing would be able to "hurt or destroy" anyone any longer, "for the earth will be full of the knowledge of the Lord as the waters cover the sea" (Isa. 11:6-9). Under this king, the Spirit would be "poured out on us," and justice would "dwell in the wilderness, and righteousness abide in the fruitful field." The people would live in a peaceful place—"in secure dwellings, and in quiet resting places"—where "the ox and the donkey range freely" (Isa. 32:15-20).

On the day of the Lord, God promised to create "new heavens and a new earth" (Isa. 65:17), renewing the Exodus—the experience of being liberated from slavery—by bringing about a new creation (see Gal. 6:15). "I have spoken, and I will bring it to pass," declared God. "I have planned, and I will do it" (Isa. 46:11). "I am God, and there is no other" (46:9). All other "works" and "images" are "empty wind" (*ruach wabohu*; 41:29), "nothing and emptiness"(*wabohu*) (40:17), like the "formless void" the Spirit (*ruach*) swept over at the beginning of creation (Gen. 1:2).

According to the word of the Lord, in God's new creation, weeping and cries of distress would cease—"former things shall not be remembered or come to mind" (Isa. 65:17). Instead, God's people would enjoy long life and the fruits of their own labor. Moreover, not only would the people rejoice on that day, but mountains and hills would also "burst into song" and "all the trees of the field . . . clap their hands" (Isa. 55:12).

The Spirit of a Messianic People

The day of the Lord would also bring internal renewal to God's people. Recall Jeremiah's hope for a time when God will make a new covenant with God's people—writing God's law on their hearts (31:33-34). Ezekiel said something similar when he declared God's promise to give the people a "new heart" and a "new spirit" within them, taking out their "heart of stone" and giving them instead "a heart of flesh." With God's Spirit within them, they would be able to keep God's statutes and carefully observe God's ordinances (Ezek. 36:26-27).

In Ezekiel 37 is recorded the prophet's shattering vision of how God's creative Spirit breathed new life into dry bones, resurrecting life from the dead. The Spirit had led him to a valley of "dry bones" of Israel's dead, as if after a brutal battle. As the prophet stood among the bones, God had him prophesy to them: "I will cause breath to enter you, and you shall live. I will lay sinews on you, and will cause flesh to come upon you, and cover you with skin" (Ezek. 37:5-6). As he prophesied, Ezekiel heard a rattling noise, as the bones started coming together, bone to its bone. There appeared sinews on the bones, and flesh and skin. When Ezekiel saw that they still were not breathing, God told him to "prophesy to the breath," and God called on the four winds to "breathe upon these slain, that they may live" (37:9). Thus breath came into them, and the bones began to stand on their feet, becoming a vast multitude of people. Precisely when the people of Israel cried out, "our bones are dried out, and our hope is lost," (37:11) God opened their graves and brought them out. God promised: "'I will put my spirit within you, and you shall live ... then you shall know that I, the Lord, have spoken and will act,' says the Lord" (37:1-14).

With equally graphic imagery, Joel anticipated the great and terrible day of the Lord—in a calamitous vision of heaven and earth covered with blood, fire, and columns of smoke. On this day, when the sun was turned to darkness and the moon to blood, God promised to "pour out my Spirit on all flesh." On that day, "your sons and your daughters shall prophesy; your old ... will dream dreams and your young ... shall see visions." Even "male and female slaves" would prophesy with the Spirit's authority (Joel 2:28).

What happens when the Spirit is "poured out on all flesh"? The Old Testament texts show that the coming of the Spirit is *universal*, falling on all people—on "all flesh." It is *total*, giving the whole person—mind, soul, and body—a "heart of flesh." It is *enduring*, a permanent resting and dwelling of the Spirit and not simply a temporary occurrence. Finally, the coming of the Spirit is *direct*, no longer mediated by tradition—by what we teach or say to each other—but grounded directly in the experience of God and God's glory.

The Spirit of God and the Human Spirit

The Spirit of God brings hope not only to the nations and the natural world, but also to us as individuals in profoundly intimate ways. The Spirit of God (*ruach Yahweh*) breathes life into us, giving us a created spirit (*ruach*). Because God's Spirit is the very breath that breathes life into our nostrils, God's Spirit is with us wherever we go and in everything we do.

> You know when I sit down and when I rise up;
> > you discern my thoughts from far away.
> You search out my path and my lying down,
> > and are acquainted with all my ways.
> Even before a word is on my tongue,
> > O Lord, you know it completely.
> You hem me in, behind and before,
> > and lay your hand upon me. (Ps. 139:2-6)

God's Spirit is always intimately related to everything that is happening in our lives, as intimate with us as the very air we breathe! God's Spirit is there when we surrender to God's will for our lives: "Into your hand I commit my spirit" (Ps. 31:5). And God's Spirit is there when we do not surrender and are not faithful to God, when we are like those "whose heart was not steadfast, whose spirit was not faithful to God" (Ps. 78:8). God's Spirit is always there, helping us to understand that we are to fear only God, since God's power is more powerful than any other power, human or otherwise, that would seek to control or oppress us.

God's Spirit is there when we sin and repent of our sin. Like the psalm attributed to David when he repented of adultery and murder, we too can cry out,

Create in me a clean heart, O God,
    and put a new and right spirit within me.
Do not cast me away from your presence,
    and do not take your holy spirit from me.
Restore to me the joy of your salvation,
    and sustain in me a willing spirit. (Ps. 51:10-12)

In the midst of our brokenness, God's Spirit helps us understand that the only "sacrifice acceptable to God is a broken spirit" and that God never despises such "a broken and contrite heart" (Ps. 51:17). God's Spirit is there when we are so distressed and afflicted—when our souls refuse to be comforted—that all we can do is lament and cry out (see Ps. 77:1-3). God's Spirit is there when our spirits faint, helping us to find a path, even when others betray us and seek to destroy us (Ps. 142:3). In these times, we can rely on God's promise to be "near to the brokenhearted" and to save "the crushed in spirit" (Ps. 34:18). God's Spirit is there even when we feel forsaken by God (Ps. 22:1). Because of this, we can confidently cry out, "Answer me quickly, O Lord; my spirit fails. Do not hide your face from me. . . . Let your good spirit lead me on a level path" (Ps. 143:7, 10).

We can, like Job, cry out "in the anguish of my spirit," complaining in "the bitterness of my soul" (Job 7:11), when "my spirit is broken . . . the grave is ready for me" (Job 17:1). We too can claim—like Job did, in his time of affliction and oppression, when even God seemed to be hiding—the promise that God's "care has preserved my spirit" (Job 10:12). Indeed, with every breath we take, we can affirm that the "spirit of God has made me, and the breath of the Almighty gives me life" (Job 33:4). In spite of our affliction and our seemingly godforsaken state, in all that happens to us we can remain faithful to the God who continually—in every moment—gives us the very breath that sustains our life: "As long as my breath is in me and the spirit of God is in my nostrils, my lips will not speak false-hood, and my tongue will not utter deceit (Job 27:3-4).

For Reflection and Discussion

1. What does the Old Testament tell us about how the Spirit is at work in our personal lives? In our communities and societies? In the natural world?

2. What do we learn by tracing the ways the understanding of the Spirit's work evolved in the Old Testament? How does messianic hope arise, and what are the main characteristics of the new age the Spirit will usher in?

2

The Spirit of God in Jesus

Something happened after Jesus' crucifixion. His followers not only experienced his presence among them as one raised from the dead, but they also experienced the presence of the Spirit the prophets had anticipated within and among them. They found themselves transported into the age of the Spirit the prophets had expected. As they asked themselves, "What is happening to us?" they realized that Jesus of Nazareth, the man from Galilee who had been crucified by religious and political authorities, was nothing other than the Messiah anointed by God's Spirit to usher in God's reign for all people.

But, if, indeed, the crucified Jesus was the exalted Messiah, how was the Spirit present and active in his life? What was his experience of God? How did the Spirit "anoint" him with such a sense of identity and mission that people felt God's coming reign was being enacted in his very presence when he was among them?

The Spirit in Jesus' Baptism

Before he began his public work as an itinerant prophet, teacher, and healer, Jesus went to John to be baptized. Dressed in camel's hair with a leather belt around his waist, John was a "baptizer" who called people to repent and be baptized in the Jordan River so that their sins might be forgiven (Mark 1:1-8). When Jesus was baptized by John, something dramatic happened. The heavens were "torn open" and the Spirit descended on him "like a dove" (Mark 1:9-10). "And a voice came from heaven, 'You are my Son, the Beloved; with you I am well pleased'" (Mark 1:11)—words that echoed the way King David was chosen as God's "son" to rule over Israel (see Ps. 2:7).

What does this mean? Jesus was God's chosen child and anointed with the Spirit's power. His baptism was a baptism into a life that would culminate in a "cup of suffering" (Mark 10:38): "For the Son of Man came not to be served but to serve, and give his life as a ransom for many" (Mark 10:45). A ransom in the ancient world was given to release or redeem someone from a situation of oppression—for example, from slavery. After his death, Jesus' followers used this metaphor to describe how, like God's chosen Servant in Isaiah, Jesus bore the diseases and sins of many, giving people a new life of forgiveness and healing in exchange for all that oppressed them (see Isa. 52:13–53:1).

The Spirit and Jesus' Temptations

Immediately after his baptism, the Spirit sent Jesus into the desert. There, the devil challenged him with three temptations. Each one tested whether Jesus would use his spiritual power in a way that was faithful to his call as God's chosen one.

Tempting him with *bodily desires and needs*, the devil told him to turn bread into stone. To this, Jesus responded, "One does not live by bread alone" (Matt. 4:4; Deut. 8:3). Tempting him to manipulate his *spiritual power* for his own purposes, the devil told him to fall down and ask the angels to save him. To this Jesus responded, "Do not put the Lord your God to the test" (Matt. 4:7; Deut. 6:16). Tempting him with *political power*, the devil showed him all the nations of the world and told him that they would all be under his power, if only he would worship the devil. To this Jesus responded, "Worship the Lord your God, and serve only him" (Matt. 4:10; Deut. 6:13).

The Spirit and Jesus' Birth

In the stories of Jesus' birth, as recorded in Matthew and Luke, the Holy Spirit "overshadows" Mary in the same way God's glory appeared in a cloud to the Israelites (see Luke 1:35; Exod. 13:21). In this way, Jesus is conceived not by a human father, but by the power of the Holy Spirit. Mary rejoiced with a hymn of praise (traditionally called the Magnificat) that echoed Hannah's words when she found herself pregnant with the prophet Samuel (see Luke 1:46-55; 1 Sam. 2:1-10). Anticipating what would happen in Jesus' life and ministry, she praised God for bringing down the mighty and raising the lowly, for filling the hungry and sending the rich away.

What do these stories mean? Telling us that God alone is the Father of Jesus Christ and that the Spirit of God indwells Jesus' humanity from his very conception, they highlight what early Christians experienced in their encounter with the risen Jesus. God had sent God's only Son to save the world (John 3:16; Rom. 8:32). As the Word who was God and was with God from eternity, Jesus—God's Son—became flesh and lived among us (John 1:1-18).

These stories also resonate with what happens to us when we too are adopted as God's children and are anointed with God's Spirit. What Jesus gives us, as human spirits, is his life-giving Spirit (1 Cor. 15:45). By faith in Jesus, we too have power to become children of God (John 1:12). Given birth by the Spirit, we too are "born anew" (John 3:1-8). God sends the Spirit of his Son into our hearts. When we cry "Abba! Father!" it is that very Spirit bearing witness with our spirits that we are, indeed, children of God—and therefore heirs of God and heirs of Christ (Gal. 4:6). But this means that we too are baptized into Jesus' "cup of suffering." We too are called to follow him by taking up our own cross (Rom. 8:16-17; Mark 8:34-37).

The Spirit and the Kingdom of God

"Filled with the Spirit," Jesus went from town to town, forgiving sins, healing those who were sick and tormented by demons, and announcing to the world: "The time is fulfilled, and the kingdom of God has come near; repent, and believe in the good news" (Mark 1:15). What was the kingdom of God Jesus proclaimed in the power of the Spirit? In what ways did Jesus embody the message of the coming kingdom of God?

Jesus proclaims good news to the poor

In Luke's version of the "Sermon on the Plain," Jesus blessed the poor and those who hungered and mourned. He also warned those who were rich, who were full and happy now (Luke 6:17-26; see also Matt. 7:1-5). When the expected kingdom of God is enacted in our midst, God raises up the lowly and brings down the mighty in our societies. Very real reversals of who has power and who does not have power take place.

Jesus speaks and acts with authority and power

As John the baptizer anticipated the coming of the kingdom of God with his calls for repentance and judgment, so Jesus, empowered by the Spirit, embodied the coming of the kingdom of God with his very presence. When John's disciples came to ask Jesus if he was the one they had been expecting, Jesus said, "Go and tell John what you hear and see: the blind receive their sight, the lame walk, the lepers are cleansed, the deaf hear, the dead are raised, and the poor have good news brought to them" (Matt. 11:4-5).

Jesus came with the "Spirit and fire" (Luke 3:16), and in his presence mighty deeds (*dunameis)* were enacted. He brought about the expected kingdom of God—the "new creation" (Gal. 6:15). And, Jesus spoke and acted with an unusual authority (*exousia).* When he walked along the road, people were filled with awe; some were even afraid of him (Mark 10:32). People were "astonished" at the way he taught, because, unlike experts in the law or the tradition, he taught with an authority that was not of "human origin" (Mark 11:28; Luke 4:22; Matt. 7:28).

Jesus exorcises demons

In Mark, it is the demons, the "unclean spirits," who first recognized that Jesus was the "Son of God" (see Mark 1:21-28; 3:11; 5:2-7). Luke records that a wild, mass phenomenon took place when Jesus started healing people and demons also came out of many of them, crying, "You are the the Son of God!" (Luke 4:40-41). When accused of having the power of "Beelzebul" (probably a reference to Satan, the ruler of demons), Jesus responded that Satan would be dividing his own kingdom if he cast out demons. However, he said, "if it is by the Spirit of God that I cast out demons, then the kingdom of God has come to you" (Matt. 12:28).

According to Jesus, although all kinds of sins and blasphemies would be forgiven, blasphemy against the Holy Spirit would not be forgiven (Mark 3:28-29; Matt. 12:31-32; Luke 12:10). What did he mean by this? Jesus' healings and exorcisms were signs of the binding of the powers of evil that would come with the messianic age. Jesus' miracles were as epochal as the miracles of Exodus and announced a new age. To deny the Spirit's activity in this new era—an activity that happens right before one's eyes—was the unpardonable sin.

Jesus forgives sins

The Gospels record many instances where Jesus forgave the sins of those who came to him. After forgiving the sins of a paralyzed man, Jesus was questioned how he could do this, since only God could forgive sins. Jesus simply answered, "The Son of Man has authority on earth to forgive sins," and told the man to stand up, take up his mat, and return home (Mark 2:3-12). In another story, a woman with a reputation for being a sinner joined Jesus as he was eating at the home of a Pharisee. With an expensive jar of oil, she stood behind Jesus, and, crying, started kissing his feet, bathing them with her tears and the oil. When the Pharisee and his friends were dismayed by this, Jesus rebuked them, saying, "her sins, which were many, have been forgiven . . . she has shown great love" (Luke 7:36-50).

Jesus heals the sick

People brought to Jesus those who suffered from all kinds of diseases—paralysis, epilepsy, leprosy, blindness, deafness, and many others. There were mass healings as well as individual healings. Jesus healed Peter's mother-in-law, a leper, a paralytic, a man with a withered hand—the list goes on. In most of these stories, the power that enacted the healing came from Jesus alone. But, in at least nine of the stories, *the faith of those healed* played an important role in the healing that took place. When Bartimaeus came to Jesus to regain his sight, Jesus told him, "Go; your faith has made you well" (Mark 10:52). When a father asked Jesus whether he was able to help his mute, epileptic son, Jesus responded, "If you are able!—All things can be done for the one who believes." And when the father cried out—"I believe; help my unbelief!"—Jesus healed his son (Mark 9:14-29).

Jesus even commended Gentiles for their faith, telling a Samaritan leper, "Your faith has made you well" (Luke 17:11-19), and a Roman centurion, who asked Jesus to heal his servant from afar, "Let it be done for you according to your faith" (Matt. 8:13). He also commended the faith of women. A woman who had been hemorrhaging for years was healed when she touched Jesus. Discovering that power had gone out of him, Jesus simply said, "Daughter, your faith has made you well" (Mark 5:34). But when a Canaanite woman came to Jesus begging him to cure her daughter tormented by a demon, Jesus replied that he was sent only for the Jews. The woman's response, "Yet even the dogs eat the crumbs that fall from their masters' table," moved Jesus greatly—perhaps even redefining the scope of his ministry—and he said to her, "Great is your faith! Let it be done for you as you wish" (Matt. 15:21-28). Faith is important! When his disciples, who had not been able to cast out an unclean spirit, inquired of him why this was so, Jesus responded: "Because of your little faith. . . ." But, he went on to say that they could move mountains with faith only the size of a mustard seed (Matt. 17:19-20).

What kind of salvation does Jesus bring? The kingdom of God heals our bodies and minds and brings good news to the poor—the good news of God's justice and mercy to all who are oppressed in some way. Regardless of their prior status, those who hear Jesus' words, and trust in his message, have a new sense of dignity and a new sense of worth. They can stand up for themselves and deal with whatever it is in their life that oppresses them.

We do not have to believe in a separate world of spirits, as the ancients did, to see that there is evil and suffering in the world. There are powers and forces in the world that destroy life—physically, psychologically, economically, politically, and so on. Even today, people find themselves in the grip of dependencies or possessed by forces, whether as individuals or as communities and societies, that can cause them to think and act in ways highly destructive to themselves and to others. The salvation Jesus brings not only heals us, but it also de-demonizes the world, liberating creation from all the powers of death that would destroy it.

Thus, Jesus power to heal cannot be separated from his power to forgive sins. The two go together. Healing does away with illness and creates health. "But salvation in its full and completed form is the annihilation of the power of death and the raising of men and women to eternal life."[1] Healings are signs, on this side of death, of God's power of resurrection, while salvation fulfills these signs with the raising of the dead to eternal life. Ultimately, Jesus' power to save the world is manifest not through his power to work miracles but through the power of his wounds—his dying as a ransom for many (see Isaiah 53). This is the ultimate meaning of his being anointed with the Spirit at baptism, the ultimate meaning of what it means for him to be God's Son.

The Community of Jesus Gathers

People were attracted to Jesus because of what he did and said. The vitality of the movement around Jesus centered on the way the coming kingdom of God came near in his presence. This movement has been described as being *charismatic* (because of its rooting in spiritual power) and *eschatological* (because it enacted the power of the coming kingdom of God). Unlike the rabbis, Jesus' relationship to his disciples did not revolve around learning a tradition. Unlike the Zealots, who were concerned with the political overthrow of Israel's oppressors, Jesus' movement was about the coming of God's kingdom, which was not defined solely in political terms. Unlike the Essenes, who were a closed community with a distinct organization and entry requirements, Jesus' movement centered on his person, and the power of the kingdom of God he embodied, and not on a set of practices. The vitality of this movement depended solely on *Jesus*, the kingdom of God enacted in his presence.

To a group of fishermen, Jesus said, "Follow me," and I will teach you to "fish for people" (Mark 1:16). To a rich man, he said, "Sell what you own, and give the money to the poor" (Mark 10:21). To a scribe who wanted to follow him wherever he went, Jesus said, "Foxes have holes, and birds of the air have nests; but the Son of Man has nowhere to lay his head" (Matt. 8:20). To someone who wanted Jesus to wait until he had buried his parents, Jesus replied, "Follow me, and let the dead bury their own dead" (Matt. 8:22). And, after disclosing to his followers that he would suffer, die, and be raised again as a "ransom for many," Jesus summarized what "following" him entailed: "If any want to become my followers, let them deny themselves and take up their cross and follow me. For those who want to save their life will lose it, and those who lose their life for my sake, and for the sake of the gospel, will save it" (Mark 8:31-36).

Who were Jesus' followers? To be sure, Jesus appointed twelve to proclaim his message of God's kingdom, sending them out—with no bread, no bag, and no money in their bags—to cure the sick, to cast out demons, and to raise the dead. Yet, Jesus' immediate circle included more than "the twelve" (who symbolize the eschatological renewal of the twelve tribes of Israel). It included, for example, a number of women, among others. And, there was no clear sense of a hierarchy or organizational structure in the movement around Jesus—no one was to be called "rabbi," "instructor," or "Father." The only criterion for measuring greatness in this group appears to have been that whoever wanted to be great must first be a servant. Whoever wanted to be "first" must be "last of all" and "servant of all" (Mark 9:35).

The movement around Jesus was characterized by openness. From Jesus' perspective, his "family" included anyone who did the will of God: "Whoever does the will of God is my brother and sister and mother" (Mark 3:35). Jesus spent much of his time in conversations with people who came to him—frequently in homes around meals—with a variety of questions and pressing needs. And, his many conversation partners included people from all sorts of backgrounds—men and women, Jews and Gentiles, Pharisees and scribes, tax collectors and sinners, the rich and the poor, both the sick and those who were well.

Indeed, Jesus was frequently reproached for having meals with tax collectors and sinners. Tax collectors were despised for collaborating with Roman oppressors, for their frequent dishonesty, and for their contact with Gentiles; and sinners were those who, in contrast to the "righteous," flouted Jewish law in some way. But when reproached, for example, for eating with a tax collector, Jesus simply responded: "Those who are well have no need of a physician, but those who are sick; I have come to call not the righteous but sinners" (Mark 2:17). Unlike John the baptizer, who was criticized for being too severe, Jesus was accused of enjoy eating and drinking too much—even of being "a glutton and a drunkard"! (Matt. 11:19).

By eating and drinking with tax collectors and sinners, Jesus embodied in his own person what the kingdom of God is like. The experience of the kingdom of God in our midst is like being invited to a great feast, where all—both good and bad—are nourished. Jesus thought of the kingdom of God as a great eschatological feast—a feast of rich food and well-aged wines, a feast that celebrates God's swallowing up of death forever and wiping away his people's tears and shame (see Isa. 25:6-10). In his parable of the great marriage feast, Jesus compared the kingdom of God to a wedding banquet, where, after the invited guests have turned down the invitation to the banquet with various excuses, the host has his servants invite everyone they can find in the streets—"the poor, the crippled, the blind, and lame" (Luke 14:21)—so that the wedding hall is filled with guests, including "both good and bad" (Matt. 22:10).

And at his Last Supper with his disciples, Jesus, the giver of the feast, was himself the gift of the feast. Here, he truly was "the kingdom of God in person"—when he offered the loaf of bread, saying, "Take; this is my body," and the cup of wine, "This is my blood of the covenant, which is poured out for many" (Mark 14:22-24). When we continue to celebrate this meal, we continue to celebrate the way the kingdom of God comes into our midst in his crucified and raised presence among us.

Jesus' Relationship with His "Abba"

People were attracted to Jesus because of what they experienced in his presence: the coming kingdom of God—the plenitude of the Spirit's power—drawing near. What the Spirit gave Jesus was a profound sense of his intimacy with God. He not only called God *Father* (with all that the word implies in the Hebrew tradition of "absolute tenderness and authority"), but he also called God *Abba* (an even more intimate form of address for a father), indicating a profound sense of being cared for by God—that he was loved, that he was wanted, that he was seen for who he was, that his needs would be met, that he would not be betrayed, that he was safe. Thus, Jesus frequently went off, away from the crowds, to be alone with his Father in prayer, leaving early in the morning or even spending much or the whole night in prayer alone (Mark 1:35; 14:32-42;

Luke 6:12). And his teaching on prayer encouraged his followers to have the same kind of intimacy he had with his father. Prayers were to be simple—without a lot of empty phrases or many words—"for your Father knows what you need before you ask him" (Matt. 6:8). The Lord's Prayer, for example, simply begins by acknowledging God's holiness and asking for the coming of the kingdom of God. Then it makes three requests: that God meet our basic needs; that God forgive our sins as we forgive those who sin against us; and that God save us from temptation (see Matt. 11:9-13).

And yet, Jesus urged his followers to have an astonishing boldness in prayer: "Have faith in God . . . believe that what you say will come to pass, it will be done for you" (Mark 11:22-23); "All things can be done for the one who believes" (Mark 9:23); "Ask, and it will be given you; search, and you will find; knock, and the door will be opened for you" (Luke 11:9). Indeed, he said, in your prayers, be like a persistent friend who comes to you at midnight and asks to borrow three loaves of bread for visitors who have arrived. Even if you do not feel like getting up to give him the bread, you will do so simply to get this friend to stop bothering you (Luke 11:5-8). Or, be like an unjust judge—who neither fears God nor respects anyone else—who grants a persistent widow justice against her opponent simply to get her to stop bothering him (Luke 18:1-8).

Further, Jesus taught his disciples to avoid being hypocritical with their prayers. When you pray, he said, do not be like hypocrites, who like to pray in public places so that they can be seen by others. "But whenever you pray, go into your room and shut the door and pray to your Father who is in secret" (Matt. 6:6). Likewise, Jesus encouraged humility in prayer. According to Jesus, the Pharisee, who thanked God that he was not like other people—rogues, thieves, adulterers, or even "this tax collector"—was less of an example of how to pray than the tax collector, who was so ashamed that he could not even look up to heaven, but beat his breast saying, "God, be merciful to me, a sinner!" (Luke 18:10-14).

Finally, Jesus encouraged forgiveness in prayer: "Whenever you stand praying, forgive, if you have anything against anyone; so that your Father in heaven may also forgive you your trespasses" (Mark 11:25). We are to love our enemies and pray for those who persecute us, since God makes the "sun rise on the evil and on the good, and sends rain on the righteous and on the unrighteous" (Matt. 5:45).

Jesus' prayers to his "Abba" reached a depth of intensity right before his arrest and crucifixion. "Distressed and agitated," and "deeply grieved," his prayer in Gethsemane expressed the complexity of what he felt. Although he asked his Father (knowing that with God "all things are possible") to "remove this cup from me," he nonetheless surrendered to God's will: "not what I want, but what you want" (Mark 14:32-36). And when he was crucified alongside two bandits for the charge of claiming to be a Messiah—"King of the Jews"—he was in such anguish that all he could do was cry out: "My God, my God, why have you forsaken me?" (Mark 15:34). Where is the Spirit in this cry of godforsakenness? To answer this, we turn to the next chapter.

For Reflection and Discussion

1. What does Jesus' being anointed with the Spirit and identified as God's beloved Son tell us about his identity and mission in the world? How was his baptism related to the death he was going to suffer? What does this tell us about the character of the Spirit's power?

2. What are the main characteristics of the kingdom of God Jesus proclaimed and enacted in his life? What does this kingdom tell us about the character of the Spirit's power?

3

The Spirit of Christ in Community

Something happened after Jesus' death. His disciples experienced his presence among them as one *raised from the dead*. They announced that God had vindicated him by raising him from the dead, making him both "Lord and Messiah" (Acts 2:36). And, they experienced the presence of the Spirit within and among them. They affirmed that the same Spirit of God who raised Jesus from the dead also dwelled within them and gave life to their mortal bodies (Rom. 8:11). As they reflected on their memories about Jesus in light of the Scriptures and what they remembered about his life, they interpreted Jesus' death to be something he offered through "the eternal Spirit"—the indestructible life of God—so that they could, with clean consciences, worship the living God (Heb. 9:14).

Something had happened not only to Jesus, but to them as well! What did they experience? How were their experiences of the risen Jesus related to their experiences of the Spirit? And how were their experiences similar to, or different from, Jesus' experience of the Spirit?

The Sending of the Spirit in Acts

In addition to experiencing the risen Jesus, his disciples were commissioned to proclaim "repentance and forgiveness of sins . . . in his name to all nations" (Luke 24:47). This commissioning was accompanied by a baptism that—unlike John's baptism only with water—would come with the Holy Spirit: "You will receive power when the Holy Spirit has come upon you; and you will be my witnesses in Jerusalem, in all Judea and Samaria, and to the ends of the earth" (Acts 1:8). Soon after this commissioning, Jesus was lifted up into heaven in a cloud (what the tradition has called the "ascension"), and, as he promised, the Spirit came upon the disciples during the Jewish festival of Pentecost.

What happened at Pentecost? There was a sound like the rush of a violent wind and divided tongues, looking like fire, that appeared among a group of disciples. Filled with the Spirit, they began to speak in languages spoken by the Jews from the Diaspora who had come to Jerusalem to celebrate Passover. A crowd gathered, and as people heard their own languages spoken, they were amazed—although some sneered, saying that the disciples were simply drunk with the wine used to enhance the ecstasy of prophets. But Peter stood up and, his voice raising, addressed the crowd:

> These are not drunk, as you suppose. For it is only nine o'clock in the morning. No, this is what was spoken through the prophet Joel:
>
> "In the last days it will be, God declares,
> that I will pour out my Spirit upon all flesh,
>   and your sons and your daughters shall prophesy,
> and your young men shall see visions,
>   and your old men shall dream dreams.
> Even upon my slaves, both men and women,
>   in those days I will pour out my Spirit;
>   and they shall prophesy" (Acts 2:28-32).

Not only had God vindicated Jesus, a righteous martyr, by raising him from the dead, but in doing so, death itself had been overcome! With the event of Pentecost, the new age of the Spirit had arrived.

Jesus was the Messiah the people had been waiting for! Although only God knew when and how Jesus would restore Israel's political hopes, the resurrection and the sending of the Spirit were signs that God's redemption had now come for all people.

The response to the gospel message

When the crowd heard Peter's message, they were "cut to the heart" (Acts 2:37). "Brothers, what should we do?" they asked the apostles. Peter replied, "Repent, and be baptized every one of you in the name of Jesus Christ so that your sins may be forgiven; and you will receive the gift of the Holy Spirit" (2:38). And those who welcomed the message were baptized, and three thousand persons are added to the group of Jesus' followers.

Four things happened when people responded to the message about Jesus, although not always in the same order. They are (1) *baptized* in the name of Jesus, a baptism that is accompanied not only with water, but also with the (2) *gift of the Holy Spirit.* Baptism is a ritual that enacts (3) *repentance*—turning one's life around—and (4) the *forgiveness of sins.* This is why the message about Jesus is so revolutionary. It is about transformation—having one's life turned around. The proclamation of the gospel is a generative event that creates something new! Baptism in the name of Jesus involves the Spirit and the fire of Pentecost. In baptism, we too receive the same Spirit, who enabled Jesus to speak with boldness and do extraordinary things.

Did the gift of the Spirit always follow baptism in Jesus' name? Although Luke clearly presupposed that Jesus' baptism was accompanied with the "Spirit and with fire" (Luke 3:16), the two did not always happen at the same time or in the same order in Acts. When Philip preached in Samaria, new converts were first baptized "in the name of Jesus" and only afterward—after the laying on of hands—did they receive the Holy Spirit (Acts 8:16-17). Likewise, when Paul found some disciples in Ephesus, he discovered that they had only been baptized into John's baptism. So, he baptized them "in the name of Jesus" and then laid hands on them so that they could receive the Holy Spirit, and they began to speak in tongues and prophesy (Acts 19:1-6). But when Peter preached in Cornelius' household, new converts first received the Holy Spirit, speaking in tongues and praising God, and were only baptized afterwards (Acts 10:44-48).

And, did the gift of tongues have to accompany the gift of the Spirit? Not necessarily. In addition to Pentecost, Peter's experience with Cornelius' household and Paul's experience with the disciples in Ephesus are the only two incidents where speaking in tongues occurred in Acts. Nonetheless, there is no denying that the experience of the Spirit was clearly charismatic and often accompanied by "signs and wonders."

Throughout Acts, we read how members of the new community were "filled with the Spirit" to move and act in certain ways. The Spirit directed the affairs of the community (Acts 5:3, 9:31), guiding through prophetic utterance (Acts 11:28; 13:2; 20:23; 21:4, 11) and through mutual discernment (Acts 15:28). And the Spirit gave individuals power to perform certain tasks for the community. They took care of the community's distribution of food to the poor (Acts 6:1-5). They spoke with wisdom and enthusiasm (Acts 6:10; 7:55; 11:24; 18:25). They witnessed to what God had done in and through Jesus, speaking boldly, especially when they were being tested (4:8, 31; 5:32; 13:9-10). And the Spirit led them in mission beyond Jerusalem. For example, the Spirit led Philip in his encounter with the Ethiopian eunuch (Acts 8:26-39); the Spirit led Peter in his encounter with Cornelius (Acts 10:19-20; 11:12); and the Spirit led Paul and his coworkers in their various travels among the Gentiles (Acts 13:2, 4; 16:6-8; 19:21; 20:22-23).

The new community experienced many of the same things that had happened when Jesus had proclaimed the good news of God's kingdom before his death. But there was a difference between their experience of the Spirit and Jesus' experience of the Spirit. Jesus was not merely another example of a person inspired by the Spirit. Jesus was the *source* and the *reason* why the Spirit was now present within and among them. The good news the disciples now proclaimed was not simply the good news of the kingdom of God (as Jesus had proclaimed it), but the good news—the gospel message—about what God had done in Jesus' life, death, and resurrection! This was why they did all that they did *in the name of Jesus*—baptizing, healing, and suffering gladly.

A picture of the new community

What did the new community look like? They gathered together and devoted themselves to the apostles' teaching and fellowship, to the breaking of bread (following the pattern of Jesus' Last Supper), and prayers. They experienced much awe, since the apostles did many "signs and wonders" among them. They shared all things in common—selling their possessions and goods, and distributing them to all, as any had need. Day by day, they spent much time together, not only in the temple but also by breaking bread in one another's homes, eating together with glad and generous hearts. They praised God in all of this, and had the goodwill of the people around them. And day by day, God added to their number those who were being saved (see Acts 2:42-47).

Because of the centrality of Jesus to their experiences of the Spirit, teaching played a central role in the new community. The apostles consistently interpreted what was happening among them in relation to what had happened in Jesus' life, death, and resurrection. The book of Acts, for example, has many long speeches that interpret what had happened through Jesus in terms of Israel's history with God (see, for example, Peter's many speeches). Nonetheless, in his speech in Athens (at the Areopagus or Hill of Ares), where he debated with Epicurean and Stoic philosophers, Paul also interpreted Jesus' resurrection in relation to Gentile experiences of God. Drawing on ancient philosopher-poets, he referred to the "unknown god" people "search" and "grope for," and the God "in whom we live and move and have our being" (Acts 17:22-31). In other speeches made during his missionary travels, he drew on a range of arguments for interpreting what happened through Jesus, depending on what the pressing needs of the occasion demanded.

In addition to "serving the word," the new community also devoted itself to "prayer" (Acts 6:4). They frequently came together to pray and to praise God. They not only observed Jewish times of prayer (Acts 3:1), but they also met frequently in one another's houses for both regular and more spontaneous time of prayers of thanksgiving and praise. In these prayers, they appealed not only to God, but also to Jesus, whose name they invoked and whom they called "Lord." The members of this new community enjoyed their experiences of worship and being together (Acts 11:23; 13:48; 15:31). But this joy was more than the warm feeling of being together in a group; it was accompanied by a deep sense of awe over what God was doing among them (Acts 2:43-47). They had a profound confidence that the eschatological Spirit of God—as a palpable, almost physical, presence among them—was doing something profound in their midst.

Luke frequently uses the phrase "signs and wonders" to describe the life of the new community in both Jerusalem and in its missionary ventures. This phrase indicates that the first community felt they were living in "the new Mosaic era of eschatological redemption," an age that experienced the same kind of "signs and wonders" that Israel had experienced when they were liberated from slavery in Egypt.[1] What were the signs of the Spirit's power? In addition to Pentecost, we find two stories about people receiving the gift of tongues. In Samaria, members of Cornelius' household spoke in tongues as an external sign that the Spirit had been poured out on the Gentiles as well, and in Ephesus, believers spoke in tongues and prophesied after hands were laid on them.

There were also many healings. Peter healed a lame man at the "Beautiful Gate" of the temple (Acts 3:1-10). Philip healed paralysis and lameness in Samaria (Acts 8:6-7). Ananias laid his hands on Paul so that he received sight after being blinded during his conversion (Acts 9:17-18). Paul healed a lame man in Lystra (Acts 14:9-10) and someone with fever and dysentery in Malta (Acts 28:8). Even Peter's shadow healed someone (Acts 5:15), as did handkerchiefs touched by Paul (Acts 19:11-12)!

There were exorcisms, too, as when Paul ordered a spirit of divination to come out of a slave-girl, whose owners had been using her to make money for them by exploiting her ability to tell fortunes (Acts 16:16). And people were raised from the dead. Peter raised Tabitha (Acts 9:36-41), and Paul raised Eutychus (Acts 20:9-12). In addition, the book of Acts records other kinds of miracles: an angel liberated Peter from prison twice (Acts 5:19-21; 12:6-11), and Paul escaped prison because of an earthquake (Acts 16:26) and had the power to shake off a viper (Acts 28:3-6).

They shared all things in common, selling their possessions and goods, and distributing the proceeds to all, as any had need (see Acts 4:32-35). Those who owned land and houses sold them, so that they could contribute the proceeds to the community, which distributed to each as any has need. Because of this, there were no needy persons among them. Just as Jesus' power and authority was always linked with proclaiming good news to the poor, so this community's signs and wonders were accompanied by a care for the poor in their midst. Not only did they believe they were of "one heart and soul" (Acts 4:32), but this belief had profound implications for what they did with their money, property, and possessions.

In order to care for the needy among them, the community had a daily distribution of food. When conflicts arose—with some groups saying that their widows, probably the most disadvantaged portion of the population, were being neglected—the community set apart some individuals who were "full of the Spirit and of wisdom" (Acts

6:3) in order to handle the distribution of food so that others could devote themselves "to prayer and to serving the word" (Acts 6:4).

Finally, just as Jesus had spent much time simply "hanging out" with his followers, frequently having meals in their homes, so this new community also spent much time together and frequently ate together in one another's homes (Acts 2:46; 20:7; 27:35). Described as the "breaking of bread" (Acts 2:42), these meals hearkened back to Jesus' meals with his friends, especially his Last Supper with his disciples. Their fellowship (*koinonia*) with one another gave them a profound sense that the eschatological community of Israel the prophets anticipated was now happening in their midst.

And God added to their number. Jesus had promised that the Spirit would be poured out not only in Jerusalem and all Judea, but also in Samaria and "to the ends of the earth" (Acts 1:8). Thus, the ecstatic experience of the Spirit being poured out at Pentecost—in Jerusalem—was repeated when Philip preached in Samaria. There, the new converts' experience of the Spirit must have been so ecstatic that it aroused the envy of a magician named Simon, who offered money to the disciples for this kind of power (Acts 8:18-20). And, it was experienced again when the mission started to move into Gentile areas—to the ends of the earth. When Peter preached to Cornelius' household, they all received the Spirit and began to speak in tongues.

To the ends of the earth

Moreover, the Spirit transformed the community itself as it spread from being a movement within Judaism to being a movement that included Gentiles as well (without having to make them follow Jewish law). The story of the conversion of Cornelius' household exemplifies this transformation (see Acts 10). Cornelius, a Roman centurion and a devout man who prayed and gave alms to the poor, received a vision while praying in which an angel told him to invite Peter to his house. The next day, Peter had a vision in which a voice told him to kill and eat animals considered unclean by Jewish dietary laws. Just as Peter was trying to interpret his puzzling dream, Cornelius's men came to tell him that Cornelius wanted a visit from him. Compelled by the Spirit, Peter arrived at his house where he gave a brief speech about Jesus to all the people who were gathered there. While he was speaking, the Holy Spirit fell upon all who heard "the word," and they too began to speak in tongues and praise God. Only afterward did Peter baptize them. But when reports of what happened reached the community in Jerusalem, many criticized Peter and other missionaries for eating in Gentile households.

Apostles and elders met in Jerusalem for the first Apostolic Council in order to address the question of whether and to what extent new Gentile converts needed to follow Mosaic Law. After much debate, Peter stood up and made the case, drawing on his experience at Cornelius' household, that the Holy Spirit told him "not to make a distinction between them and us" (Acts 11:12). Then Paul and Barnabas stood up and told about the signs and wonders God was doing through them among the Gentiles. Finally, James (Jesus' brother, and a central figure in the Jerusalem church) quoted the prophet Amos to argue that God had, indeed, anticipated a time when "all other peoples . . . even all the Gentiles" would call on the Lord's name (see Acts 15:12-18).

Then the apostles and the elders, with the consent of the whole church, arrived at the following conclusion in a letter that they sent to the church in Antioch: "For it has seemed good to the Holy Spirit and to us to impose on you no further burden than these essentials . . ." (Acts 15:1-35). After this council, the rest of the book of Acts chronicles Paul's missionary ventures among the Gentiles, which finally culminate with him being in Rome, where the book ends with him welcoming all who come to him—"proclaiming the kingdom of God and teaching about the Lord Jesus Christ with all boldness and without hindrance" (Acts 28:30).

The Sending of the Spirit in John

The Gospel of John is one of our other main sources for understanding what happened when Jesus sent the Spirit to his followers (see John 14:16-17, 25-26; 15:26; 16:4b-15). John has a slightly different chronology of Jesus' sending of the Spirit; it happened on the day of the resurrection. Nonetheless, the same elements are there, beginning with Jesus commissioning the disciples, "As the Father has sent me, so I send you" (John 20:21). After this, he breathed on them saying, "Receive the Holy Spirit. If you forgive the sins of any, they are forgiven them; if you retain the sins of any, they are retained" (20:22-23).

There is another main difference between Acts' account of the Spirit's work and John's account. Instead of describing all sorts of charismatic "signs and wonders," John reads much more like a mystical text, using words like *truth, know,* and *love,* and phrases like *"abides in you"* and *"will be in you"* to describe what happens when the Spirit comes. With John, the focus of the Spirit's activity was not on the miraculous spread of the gospel, but on the way the Spirit is Jesus' living presence among us, a living presence who leads us into a deeper relationship with the one Jesus calls Father. In John's Gospel most of what Jesus has to say about the Spirit is found in a farewell speech Jesus gave his disciples at the Last Supper as he anticipated his death (see John 13–17). In this speech, Jesus consoled his followers who were troubled by the fact that he would soon be leaving them. He comforted them by telling him that he would ask his Father to send them another Advocate to be with them forever (John 14:17); indeed, it was to their advantage that he go away so that he could send this Advocate to them (John 16:7). Elsewhere in this speech, the Advocate is described as one "the Father will send in my name" (John 15:26).

What is meant by the term *Advocate?* An advocate is the equivalent of a defense lawyer. The Greek word is *paraclete* (which only John uses in the New Testament), and it can be also translated as "helper" or "comforter." According to John, the Advocate is the "Spirit of truth" (John 14:17; 15:26; 16:13). Throughout, it is emphasized that Jesus is the truth, who reveals the truth of the Father to us (John 14:6); Jesus is the Father's "Word made flesh" (John 1:1-18). Just as Jesus is the truth disclosing the Father to us, so now the Advocate, the Spirit of truth, will be Jesus' living presence with us when he leaves.

As Jesus' living presence with us, the Advocate will give us a deeper and an even more expansive—a more vital and more life giving—understanding of the truth. Jesus told his disciples, the Advocate will not only "teach you everything" (14:26), but also "guide you into all the truth; . . . and . . . declare to you the things that are to come" (John 16:13). Nonetheless, what the Advocate will disclose would always be rooted in Jesus, reminding the disciples of all Jesus has said to them. The Advocate would always only "testify" on Jesus' behalf (John 15:26). Just as Jesus did not speak on his own, but only the Father's words, so the Advocate would not "speak on his own," but only "speak whatever he hears" (John 16:13)—from Jesus and the Father.

How will the Advocate guide us into all truth? The Spirit guides us into living, existential truth by abiding—dwelling or living—in us and being in us (John 15:7). Because of the Advocate, Jesus' living presence within us, we will "abide in" or "be" in Jesus—"You in me, and I in you" (John 14:20)—even after Jesus has departed. What does it mean to abide in Jesus? In his farewell speech to the disciples, Jesus described "abiding" in him in two ways. First, it is about *bearing much fruit* (John 15:7-8). As we abide in Jesus—and his words abide in us—our lives become generative, more creative, and more "fruitful." Indeed, Jesus boldly says that we can ask for whatever we wish in his name and it will be done for us. Our lives can expand; we can enter into life more fully and live in ways that embody the everlasting life that Jesus gives us (John 16:23-24).

Second, abiding in Jesus is about abiding in his love by *keeping his commandments*. And Jesus' commandment is simply that "you love one another as I have loved you" (John 15:12). As Jesus has loved us—and as the Father has loved us by sending Jesus to us—so we are to love one another (John 15:9). This is what it means to "keep [Jesus'] words" (John 14:23). Indeed, if the truth the Spirit discloses to us is Jesus' words, then these words are all about love: the command to love one another as Jesus and the Father have loved us.

Moreover, if, as Jesus said, "all that the Father has is mine" (John 16:15), then what the Spirit discloses to us is all that Jesus shares with the Father. Jesus' relationship with his Father is one of profound intimacy: "I am in the Father and the Father is in me" (John 14:10). Thus, by abiding in the Spirit in the truth, we find ourselves in the midst of the very intimacy of Jesus' relationship to his Father. In other words, the truth the Spirit guides us into is a profoundly *relational truth*—one that is deeply grounded in Jesus' relationship to his Father, the Word who is God and is with God from eternity (John 1:1-4). The Father and the Son are distinct, but profoundly related: Jesus is in the Father, and the Father is in Jesus. Likewise, although we are distinct from Jesus, when we abide in Jesus, we are in Jesus and Jesus is in us. But that also means that, through the Spirit of truth, we are not only in Jesus, but also in the midst of the *relationship* he has with his Father.

These themes are reiterated in Jesus' final prayer to the Father, which concludes his farewell speech to his disciples: "As you, Father, are in me and I am in you, may they also be in us ... that may they be one, as we are one, I in them and you in me, that they may become completely one" (John 17:21-22). Just as the Spirit of truth enables us to enter more fully into the "us" of Jesus' relationship with his Father, so this same Spirit of truth enables us to enter more fully into the "us" of our relationship with one another.

If the truth the Spirit discloses is Jesus' relationship with his Father—how they are distinct yet fully related to one another—then through our participation in that relationship, the Spirit also discloses to us how, even though we are distinct from one another, we can still fully be related to one another. Indeed, Jesus said, it is only in this way that the world—where Jesus sends us—can know the truth about Jesus and the Father, and fully understand why it is that Jesus has sent his followers into the world, as the Father has sent him into the world (John 17:16-19).

Testing the spirits

Just as the Old Testament prophets had to test true from false prophets, so too the early Christian communities had to test true from false spirits. How does one distinguish the Spirit of truth from a spirit that deceives? First John (a letter that comes out of the same community as the Gospel of John) presents two criteria for "testing the spirits." First, we know the Spirit of God is present when we confess that Jesus Christ has come in the "flesh" (1 John 4:1-5; John 1:1-18). When the Spirit of God abides in us, we are able to trust in the name of Jesus Christ, the Son God has sent into the world as a full human being like us so that we might live our lives through him (1 John 3:23; 4:19; John 3:16).

Second, we know that the Spirit of God is present when we love our brothers and sisters. Because God is love—and love is from God—everyone who loves is born of God and knows God (1 John 4:7). As those "born anew" by the Spirit who makes us children of God (John 3:1-10; 1:12), we know we are "born of God" when we have love for one another.

This love is not merely a human love. We love because God first loved us and made us God's children. Nonetheless, because God is love, those who abide in love, abide in God and God abides in them. Although we have not seen God, we know that God lives in us—and God's love is perfected in us—when we love one another.

Thus, we cannot say, "I love God," and hate our brothers and sisters. When we do this, we are liars—we are deceivers. "How does

God's love abide in anyone who has the world's goods and sees a brother or sister in need and yet refuses to help?" (1 John 3:17) asks the letter. "For those who do not love a brother or sister whom they have seen, cannot love God whom they have not seen" (1 John 4:20).

The Sending of the Spirit through Paul

Acts gives us a gripping *charismatic* account of what the new community the Spirit created looked like and how that community spread throughout the world. John gives us a profound *mystical* understanding of how the Spirit of truth enables us to enter more deeply into Jesus' relationship with his Father and our relationships with one another.

Paul brought these two themes together. Like Acts, he described, as an apostle to the Gentiles, how the Spirit ushers in a new creation for all people (Rom. 15:14-21). Like John, he described how the Spirit leads us into a deeper understanding of what it means to be children of God, bearing witness with our Spirit that we are heirs—of God and joint heirs with Christ (Gal. 4:6; Rom. 8:15-16). Moreover, Paul explored more fully how the Spirit conforms us to Christ's living presence within us—not only through his resurrection, but also through his death. For Paul, being an "heir of Christ" meant that we must also "suffer with him so that we may also be glorified with him" (Rom. 8:17).

For Reflection and Discussion

1. How is the Spirit at work in the book of Acts? What are the characteristics of the Spirit's power in the new community and how does that community spread "to the ends of the earth"?

2. How is the Spirit at work in John and 1 John? How does the Spirit of truth lead us into a deeper relationship, grounded in

love, not only with Jesus, but also with his Father and with one another?

3. How is the Spirit at work in the letters of Paul? How does the Spirit conform us to Christ's death and resurrection?

4

The Spirit Creates Faith

How do we receive the Spirit? Do you have to *do* anything to receive the Spirit? Many of us think "being spiritual" is about doing certain things, saying or thinking certain things, or feeling certain things. In his letter to the Galatians, Paul made the bold assertion that we receive the Spirit not by works—not by anything we do—but simply by faith in the promise given to us through the "good news" we have received about Jesus. What does he mean by this?

The Issue: Faith versus Works

Imagine a congregation in southern Minnesota made up of Scandinavian-Americans. Some Mexicans move into the area for work. If they start attending this congregation, what will they have in common with the Scandinavian-Americans? What will be the basis for their being in "fellowship" with one another? This is a question Christians have had to grapple with as Christianity has spread throughout the world. What is at the heart of faith in Christ? Is it a set of practices? A set of ideas and doctrines? A set of feelings?

Paul addressed this problem in his letter to the Galatians. He was angry as he wrote the letter because, in his view, some people had been perverting the gospel, confusing people, and causing them to turn way from the grace of God. He was so angry that he even wished these people would castrate themselves (Gal. 5:12)!

Why was he so incensed? Because some people were saying that Gentile converts needed to be circumcised and follow Jewish law when they became Christians. At issue was precisely the question of how one received the Spirit. Do we receive the Spirit, Paul was asking, because of our *works* or because our *faith*? Does God's power in our lives—God's power to work miracles, to transform us, and to bring about a new creation among us—rely on what we *do* or on our *faith in the promise*, the promise that comes in Jesus (Gal. 5:1-5)?

Abraham's faith, Paul argued in his letter to the Romans, was "reckoned to him as righteous." Abraham was "justified" because he had faith in God's promise. What does it mean to be justified? It simply means being made righteou*s*, being made one who is worthy of being in relationship to God, being one made worthy of being called a child of God. The promise given to Abraham was sheer gift, sheer grace. It was not "something due" him (or us). It was something received by faith alone (Rom. 4:1-11).

Why is this? In and of themselves, good works and keeping the law are good things. There is nothing inherently wrong with works or the law. In fact, as we will see, living by faith in Christ enables us to keep God's commands to love God above all else and our neighbors as ourselves. The problem with the law is that it does not have the power to *save* us. It is impotent. It merely makes distinctions: good/bad, right/wrong, lawful/unlawful, circumcised/uncircumcised. It merely points out what sin is, and what the consequences of sin are (Rom. 3:20). If you lie, steal, murder, or commit adultery, things will not go well for you. If you allow your societies to be unjust and you exploit and oppress the poor, people will suffer on a massive scale. If you live as God would have you live, you will have life; if you do not, destruction—death—will happen. But the law cannot deal with sin and the underlying destructive patterns that cause us to sin. In fact, the law turns us into divided selves. Like Paul, even though we know in our innermost selves what we ought to do, there are parts of us—parts we are often unconscious of or only dimly aware of—that keep us from doing what our consciences tell us to do (Rom. 7:14-25).

Contemporary psychology describes well what Paul was talking about when he wrote about this "other part" of our selves, which is often driven by primal instincts within us that have been deeply shaped not only by what we have done in our lives, but by what others have done to us. Driven by fear and desire, these instincts compel us to act in ways that often counter our best intentions, our best sense of who we should be and what we should do.

The letter of the law can only kill. It only points out how impotent we are in the face of destructive patterns that keep us from acting on our best intentions. It can only rob us of agency when we discover how divided we are—between our sense of what is good and right and our inability to be good and do the right thing. By contrast, "the Spirit gives life" (2 Cor. 3:6). Only God's Spirit has the power to make us righteous, to take all the parts of our selves—both good and bad, what we have control over and what we do not have control over—and transform them through Christ's life-giving Spirit.

Only the Spirit can create life out of death or any destructive pattern. Only God could make the promise that Abraham would be the "father of many nations," even though his wife was old and so far had had a barren womb. Only the God who gives "life to the dead and calls into existence the things that do not exist" can make us righteous (Rom. 4:17). This is why faith and grace are very different from law and works. Faith in God's promise gives us the power to be God's righteous children. And, unlike the law, God's grace—God's gift—has no conditions. Given freely to all, it comes out of the excess of God's infinite life and love. It is a promise available for everyone—without distinction—regardless of whether we are good or bad, male or female, slave or free person, Jew or Greek, and so on.

The best analogy for understanding this is the analogy of good parenting. Indeed, this is all about the promise of adoption and God's good parenting of us as "adopted" children. Children who know that they are cared for and respected—who know that they have inherent value in themselves regardless of what they do—often have the capacity to act freely in ways that are life-giving and not destructive. Their sense of self is secure enough to overcome basic human fears and desires so that they can lead productive and healthy lives. On the other hand, children who think they will only have their basic needs for love and respect met if they meet certain conditions (if they are good, right, competent, or successful, for example), often tend to act in ways that are governed by fundamental desires or fear. Their desires to have their fundamental needs met—or fear that these needs will not be met—tend to become compulsive "laws" within them governing what they do. These laws within them often are destructive, either to themselves or to other people, and keep them from acting out of their best sense of what is right and good.

The Exchange

God's love for us—God's *unconditional* love—has been expressed in a very concrete way. In ancient Israel, a hanged criminal had to be buried immediately so that his body would not "defile the land" (Deut. 21:23). As a hanged criminal, Jesus took on, in his own body, the "curse" of sin, the pollution of death and disease that resulted from sin and injustice. He entered into the very "nothingness" sin and injustice creates in our bodies. In his death he took on our god-forsaken condition (Mark 15:34).

Christ took on our "curse" so we could receive the "promise of the Spirit" (Gal. 3:13, 14). Christ became sin so that we could receive his righteousness (2 Cor. 5:21). This "exchange" is very different from the conditions of the law's "exchange." With the law's exchange, we are only given what is due us. By contrast, rooted in God's unconditional grace, Christ's exchange for us undoes the whole economy of the law's exchange. Where sin has abounded, grace now abounds all the more (see Rom. 5:12-18). In his letters,

Paul used all sorts of metaphors to describe what happens in this exchange. As in a law court, we are "justified," given a righteousness that is worthy of being in relationship with God. As in a slave market, we are "redeemed" and "ransomed" from all that keeps us in slavery or bondage. As with temple imagery, we are "sanctified," made holy and pure by the Spirit's life within us. As with conflicts and warfare, we are now "reconciled" with God. We and the rest of the world become a "new creation."

In this exchange, we receive Christ's life-giving Spirit. The same Spirit who raised Jesus from the dead now lives within us. The promise made to Abraham and his descendants is now made available to all people—without distinction. Echoing Joel, Paul said that the Spirit has been "poured into our hearts" (Rom. 5:5). Echoing Ezekiel, he said that the Holy Spirit has been given to us (1 Thess. 4:8). Echoing Jeremiah, he said that the Spirit has written God's law in our hearts (2 Cor. 3:4-18). Through the Spirit, we now have access to the very intimacy Jesus had with his *Abba*. God sends the Spirit of his Son into our hearts when we cry "Abba! Father!" and this Spirit bears witness with our spirit that we are, indeed, not only children of God, but heirs of all that Christ has as God's chosen Son—indeed, we are "heirs of God" (Gal. 4:6; Rom. 8:15-16).

Moreover, this exchange is not simply something that takes place in some ethereal world, in some Gnostic heaven divorced from our bodies. In our baptism into Christ, our whole selves—our minds, hearts, and bodies—have died to their old, destructive ways of being. By faith, we now live our mortal lives out of the creative power of Christ's life-giving Spirit within us (Gal. 2:20).

We now have Christ's image as the primal pattern shaping our identities. The Spirit has been poured into our hearts in order to give us the power to live out that image. This image is not another ideal—another law—to make us aware of our impotence. Christ's image is nothing like that. Rather, the power of his resurrected life, the power of his life-giving Spirit, continually creates new life within us so that we can enter into all the possibilities God has in store for us. Where the "Spirit of the Lord is, there is freedom," and through the Spirit's power we can, indeed, be "transformed into the same image [of Christ] from one degree of glory to another" (2 Cor. 3:17-18).

The paradox here is that as we grow more fully into Christ's image, we become more fully ourselves. The Spirit bears witness with our spirit that we are children of God (Rom. 8:16). We do not lose our unique individual identities when we enter into Christ's life; we do not become Christ. Rather, we become more fully ourselves. Christ's life-giving Spirit gives us the power to deal with destructive patterns in our lives—patterns that keep us trapped in destructive thoughts, feelings, and behaviors—so that we can be all that God has created us to be, so that we can, by faith, step into all the possibilities God would have for us. Where destructive patterns in our lives have abounded, now grace can abound all the more!

Moreover, this is not simply some narcissistic fantasy of our own omnipotence. In baptism, we are incorporated into the "we" of Christ's body, a body offered for all people. The same life-giving power we have by faith is gratuitously offered to everyone else. Our special sense of being "chosen" and "adopted" is something we share with all for whom Christ died. The Spirit is lavishly poured out on all people. The infinite excess of God's love shows no bounds; it makes no distinctions. In Christ there is a "new creation"; we no longer view one another in the same way (2 Cor. 5:17). Our usual ways of making distinctions among people no longer hold. By faith, we all can share in the potency of Christ's identity as chosen child (Gal. 3:28). And here we arrive at another seeming paradox. As we enter more fully into our individual potency by entering more fully into the potency of Christ's life-giving Spirit, we also enter more fully into relationships with others, more fully appreciating their own individual gifts.

The Spirit's Freedom

Faith is always about freedom. The faith the Spirit creates within us is always a faith that gives us more life and more freedom. Now, the Lord is the Spirit, and where the Spirit of the Lord is, there is freedom" (2 Cor. 3:17). The same *Yahweh* ("the Lord") who was at work liberating the people of Israel out of slavery in Egypt is now the same Spirit at work liberating us from all that keeps us from living out of God's possibilities for us. This is what the Spirit of Christ gives us. In his resurrection, all that destroys life has been overcome.

We are freed from all our compulsive and obsessive ways of being that keep us trapped in destructive patterns of behavior—from addictions of all sorts to ways of dealing with others that either dehumanize ourselves or dehumanize others. We are freed from having to pay obeisance to all the narcissists and tyrants—whether in our personal lives or in our societies—who would seek to use us merely as means for their ends. We are freed from all that oppresses us, whether in our psyches or in our societies. We can stand up and take charge of our lives.

My mother experienced this spiritual freedom as a teenager in a concentration camp in China, where her family, along with other expatriates, was interned during World War II. After she and a group of friends had been praying for some time to be released from the camp, she realized that true freedom had nothing to do with being imprisoned or not. Many others in that camp discovered the same thing (as Langdon Gilkey describes in *Shandung Compound*, a book about the camp). Because many in the camp understood this—and because in that particular internment camp, prisoners were given more latitude than in most Japanese camps—many of those interned devoted their lives to creating as much of a civil society as they could. Among these was Eric Liddell, the hero in the movie *Chariots of Fire*, who devoted his energies to working with the youth in the camp.

But this freedom is not merely a freedom to do whatever we want regardless of the consequences to ourselves or to others. Although human distinctions no longer count—between what is lawful and not lawful, between "circumcision" and "uncircumcision"—what counts now is "faith working through love" (Gal. 5:6). Indeed, Christ's life-giving Spirit enables us to fulfill God's law. The "law of the Spirit of life in Christ Jesus" (Rom. 8:2) is an unconditional and non-literal law that, through its creative power, frees us from being so gripped by our own interests and needs (and the compulsive fears and desires that often come with those needs) that we cannot attend to the needs and interests of others. Because of God's unconditional love, we are given power to fulfill the law, as summarized in a single commandment: "You shall love your neighbor as yourself" (Gal. 5:14). The love (*agape* in Greek) that faith "works out" has nothing to do with having a special feeling. It has to do simply with attending to other people's interests as much as you would to your own interests.

Since the Spirit's power is for everyone, any attempt to use it to buttress one's own interests or the interests of one's group over the interests of others would be a contradiction of its very essence. The Spirit's power cannot be manipulated or linked with any form of envy or wrangling with another. This freedom is not to be used as an opportunity for self-indulgence; it is a freedom to to enter into the generative possibilities of the Spirit's power to create life. The freedom faith gives can only be worked out in love.

But who is our neighbor? Our neighbor now includes everyone—sinners and righteous people, men and women, people of other social classes and ethnicities, even people who have different religious beliefs from us. And, what does it mean to love your neighbor as yourself? Does this kind of love call for a kind of self-sacrificial masochism? Christ was only able to give himself fully for others because he had all the power that came with being endowed with God's Spirit as God's chosen one. Likewise, we are only able to love others fully by faith, by entering fully into the power of Christ's life-giving Spirit within us.

Thus, with faith comes a profound self-love. Through the Spirit's power, we are able to love ourselves—and accept even those parts of us we are most ashamed or guilty about—precisely because God knows and loves every part of us. Indeed, it is only when we are no longer so buttressed by the incessant demands of our own fears and desires—when we can actually become an integrated rather than a divided self—that we can truly attend to what others need, that we can truly attend to their interests and not merely to our own.

Flesh versus Spirit

In his letter to the Galatians, the apostle Paul issued the call to "live by the Spirit" and "do not gratify the desires of the flesh" (Gal. 5:16). But what does Paul mean by "flesh"?

Living in the flesh

In the Bible, the "flesh" simply refers to what God has created—what is finite and transitory, not divine. As such, "flesh" is a good thing, since God created a good world. But in the contrast between "flesh" and "Spirit," flesh refers specifically to an apocalyptic conflict between two ages—the old age of destructive forces and the new age of the Spirit's creative life and power. We can think of these two ages—these two worlds—as force fields of energy. In one, we find ourselves in a force field of negative energy that destroys life. In the other, we find ourselves in a force field of positive energy that creates life—that brings forgiveness where there is sin, healing where there is disease, and life where there is death. These patterns take place within the world at large, in the conflict between the old age of the powers of evil and new age of the Spirit's creative life. But they also take place within our own lives, as we find ourselves confronted with two different ways of being in the world, two different force fields of energy in which to live our lives.

As we have said, all "flesh" is created by God and thus is inherently good. The "flesh" only becomes linked with destruction when something other than God, the source of life, becomes the center of our lives. When we place something other than God at the center—say, when we place another person or an institution, or some other aspect of finite life (like wealth, status, beauty, physical health, approval)—we make ourselves vulnerable to death. Why? Because all finite things will eventually pass away. When things other than God are at the center of our lives, we become vulnerable to the fear that we will lose these things (which, of course, we ultimately will, since they are finite). And we become vulnerable to the desires that will get us to do anything—regardless of the consequences to ourselves—to get these things.

We become caught in patterns of regret and resentment over what has happened in the past when we did not get what we wanted or needed. We fear the future, afraid that we might not get what we desire. We quarrel and fight with one another—and even go to war—to get what we want. We get caught up in factions and unnecessary conflicts in order to secure our own personal or group interests. Our lives are full of strife and conflict. We are envious and jealous, and cannot appreciate what others have. We exploit people who have less power than we do in order to get what we want, or we allow ourselves to be exploited, fearing the power others have over us. Our societies become unjust, with vast gaps between the wealthy and poor, economic instability fed by greed and fear, and political unrest. We find ourselves prey to compulsive addictions that help us avoid the pain of having to deal with the difficulties of life. We use our sexuality inappropriately, either by exploiting others to fulfill our own desires or by allowing ourselves to be exploited.

The Bible is full of lists of the things that happen when God's life-giving ways of living are no longer at the center of our lives. We also merely have to turn on the television and watch a news program to get a sense of the destructive patterns we can get ourselves into—either as individuals or as societies.

Living in the Spirit

By contrast, living in the Spirit is precisely about living out of God's creative power in our own lives. The Spirit is God's energizing power in our lives, continually working good out of whatever is happening to us or around us. Living out of the Spirit's life, we find we become more expansive and more generous. We have greater sense of our worth and the worth of others. The Spirit opens us up to new possibilities, since for God all things are possible.

Unlike wealth, success, health, or even a good reputation, the "fruit" the Spirit bears in our lives cannot be taken away from us. The things that the Spirit manifests in our lives cannot be manipulated or controlled. They cannot be manufactured. They are completely "free," for all people, with no strings attached; we need not compete for these things and be envious about them. We cannot "make" these things happen. The fruit of the Spirit comes by itself. But we can let it be and let it come.

With the Spirit, we can let go and forget our inner struggles. We can let go and forget our struggles with others too. Our hearts are open and happy. Our minds are rested. Our bodies are relaxed. With the Spirit comes awe, wonder, expansion, aliveness, and warmth. With the Spirit, we can speak with "frankness and godly sincerity, not by earthly wisdom but by the grace of God" (2 Cor. 1:12). Guided by our conscience, we speak truth buoyed by the power of God. With the Spirit, love, joy, and peace are our natural states. We are spontaneously kind, generous, and gentle. We are loyal to the people in our lives. We are instinctively patient with their foibles. Our fears and desires no longer control us (Gal. 5:22-23).

Right now, my mother, who is in a nursing home with Alzheimer's, best embodies the fruit of the Spirit for me. She used to be a very articulate woman who frequently spoke in churches and wrote books. Now she cannot even form a coherent sentence. But when I am with her, she radiates such warmth—such delight in life—that I am bathed with exquisite tenderness and sweetness. I can describe this as nothing other than the fecundity of the Spirit's life.

For Reflection and Discussion

1. Why do we receive the Spirit by faith and not by works? What does this tell us about who the Spirit is and how the Spirit works in our lives?

2. What is at the heart of the contrast between "flesh" and "Spirit"? What kind of freedom does the Spirit give us? And why—if living in the Spirit means having Christ formed in us—do we become more fully ourselves as we grow more fully into Christ's life?

5

The Spirit Creates Love

All that counts now is "faith working through love" (Gal. 5:6). But what does this mean in the face of our very real differences with one another? What does this mean in the face of our very real conflicts with one another over power?

How does faith get "worked out in love" when some people are simply more powerful than others? And the reason some have more power than others is because of differences among us—differences in personal capacities (like force of personality or individual gifts and talents) and general differences (like differences based on gender, wealth, social status, race, ethnicity, and so on).

Moreover, what do we do about the fact that profound spiritual experiences often intensify these very human tensions? Often our deepest conflicts arise because of the different ways we experience the Spirit in our lives. The history of Christianity is a record not only of experiences of Christ's Spirit within and among us, but also of our conflicts over power—conflicts over our use of spiritual power and our use of human power.

The book of Acts gives us a glowing account of the spread of Christianity, but it does not really give us criteria for discerning appropriate uses of spiritual power. The Johannine literature gives us criteria for "testing the spirits," but it does not help us deal with differences among us. We turn to Paul's first letter to the Corinthians to get some insight into these issues. A prosperous urban center within the Roman Empire, Corinth was ethnically, culturally, and religiously diverse. The Corinthian congregation probably reflected the diversity within the city itself.

And this congregation was rife with conflict and dysfunction. Some had had spiritual experiences that made them feel superior to others. Rival factions were jockeying for control. The needs of poorer members of the congregation were being ignored. Some members were being flagrantly immoral in their sexual behavior; others were engaged in lawsuits with one another. There were conflicts over the status of women and conflicts over basic Christian beliefs. The list could go on. In the midst of all of this, Paul wrote a letter appealing for reconciliation.

Christ, the Wisdom and Power of God

Paul based his appeal for reconciliation on the message of the cross. Mark's Gospel explicitly related Jesus' statements about the suffering and crucifixion he was about to experience to conflicts the disciples were having are having over who was the "greatest" among them. Likewise, Paul's letters to the Corinthians explicitly relate the message of the cross to conflicts over power within the Corinthian congregation. Conflicts over power are the "setting in life" (what scholars call the *Sitz im Leben*) that the message of the cross addresses.

Factions within the Corinthian congregation had aligned themselves with various strong leaders: "I belong to Paul," or "I belong to Apollos" or, "I belong to Cephas,"—or even, "I belong to Christ" (1 Cor. 1:12). To this, Paul, the quintessential theologian of the cross, simply said that he had been called "to proclaim the gospel, and not with eloquent wisdom, so that the cross might not be emptied of its power" (1 Cor. 1:17). What was the message of the cross? Jesus' crucifixion was a source of embarrassment for Jews who expected the "signs" of a Messiah who would overthrow Israel's oppressors. And, the cross was sheer "foolishness" to the Greeks who respected leaders who were able to establish and maintain their political power. Jesus' death was a conundrum to the Jewish scribe, the Roman rhetor, and the Greek sage. Yet, this event was the very means by which

God created a new humanity out of not only Jews and Greeks, but men and women, and slaves and free people (Gal. 3:28). The cross manifests God's power and God's wisdom, a power and a wisdom that radically subverts our usual human conceptions of power and wisdom (1 Cor. 1:18-25).

Who hears this message? Instead of calling those who were wise by human standards, or powerful, or of noble birth, God chose what was foolish and weak to shame the wise and the strong. God chose what was "low and despised in the world, things that are not, to reduce to nothing things that are" (1 Cor. 1:27-28). And who speaks this message? I proclaim the mystery of God, Paul said, not in lofty words or plausible wisdom. I came in weakness and in fear and in much trembling. "For I decided to know nothing among you but Jesus Christ, and him crucified," and my speech and proclamation comes with nothing but "a demonstration of the Spirit and of power, so that your faith might rest not on human wisdom but on the power of God" (1 Cor. 2:1-5).

What the message of the cross proclaims is that God is the source of our life together in Christ. Because of what God has done through Christ, Christ now embodies God's wisdom for us. Christ now embodies our righteousness. Christ now embodies our sanctification. Christ now embodies our redemption. We are given a new way of perceiving and responding to life, a new way of "boasting" about ourselves—of singing our praises—one not based on human wealth, wisdom, or might, but solely on God's "steadfast love, justice, and righteousness" (Jer. 9:24).

The Spirit and True Maturity

We are like immature children—competing siblings—when we quarrel and are jealous of one another. But with the Spirit's power, we can mature. We can become less egocentric and more considerate of others. The kind of power the Spirit gives us is very different from the kind of power the "rulers of this age" wield. They can only understand power as something you either fear in others, or use to control them. If they understood what God's power is all about—the power manifest in the message of the cross—Jesus would not have needed to be crucified (1 Cor. 2:6-8).

Unlike other things we see, hear, feel, or touch, the Spirit's power is not something we can grasp or comprehend. God is Spirit and can only be worshiped in Spirit and in truth (John 4:24). Only the Spirit grasps and comprehends what is truly God's; only the Spirit searches everything, even the depths of God (1 Cor. 2:10-11). Those who merely rely on their natural capacities (the *psychikoi*) cannot understand what the Spirit teaches. Only those who rely on the Spirit (the *pneumatikoi*) can understand what the Spirit teaches. And what the Spirit forms within us is Christ's mind (*nous*), a way of viewing life that always has the cross as its lens for interpreting things. From the standpoint of Christ's life-giving Spirit, we truly can become mature adults, who are aware not only of their own needs but also of the needs of others.

Maturing in the Spirit is like working in a garden with others. One person plants, another waters, but both work for a common purpose. Or, it is like working on a construction project: one group lays the foundation, another group builds on it, but both groups have a shared goal. Only what is of value—what builds the Spirit's work among us—is going to be of lasting value in what we build together. The Spirit burns away everything else.

As we mature, we see that all of us are the temple of the Spirit— that we, both as individuals and as communities, are the place where the Spirit dwells. We must not do anything that would destroy others, or ourselves, because we are God's temple and God's temple is holy. Indeed, from the vantage point of the Spirit's life within us, we can see that "all things" are ours. Not only do our various leaders belong to us, as well as factions they represent, but also life and death, along with all of time—past, present, and future. "All belong to you, and you belong to Christ, and Christ belongs to God" (1 Cor. 3:23).

Spiritual Gifts for the Common Good

Like other ancient writers, Paul used the body as a metaphor to illustrate how unity among people can be compatible with diversity. In our baptism, we are all baptized into one body—Christ's body—and we all receive the same Spirit. We all share in this body, whether we are Jew or Greek, slave or free, or male and female (1 Cor. 12:13). From now on, we regard no one from a human point of view—from the standpoint of our human distinctions (2 Cor. 5:16). Our unity in Christ's body, however, does not mean a loss of individuality, a loss of difference. Rather, our differences now are based on the gifts (*charisma*) the Spirit gives each of us to contribute to the body of Christ.

There are varieties of gifts—varieties of services and varieties of activities—that the Spirit activates or energizes within each of us. Each one of us is given gifts to contribute to the common good. Each one of us is given a specific "manifestation of the Spirit" for the benefit of all. These *charisma* are different from the "gift of the Spirit" with which God endows all believers when we enter Christ's life. These *charisma* have to do with particular services or activities we have each been given in order to make a specific contribution to a community (much like the *charisma* leaders and prophets in ancient Israel received for specific tasks).

You know what a delight it is to perform some task you are uniquely qualified to enact, whether within your family or at your place of work or within the church. As we mature in the Spirit's life, we become more fully ourselves. We become more fully aware of how we are different from others, and we become more aware of how our differences in fact can make important contributions to the communities to which we belong. Paul included two lists of gifts in his letter to the Corinthians (see 1 Corinthians 12). We often tend to ignore the first list, because it presents activities we in the Western world tend to devalue. On the one hand, it includes gifts dealing with the capacity to discern what needs to be said at a particular point in time: the utterance of wisdom, the utterance of knowledge, prophecy, and the discernment of spirits (1 Cor. 12:8-10).

All of these gifts have to do with speaking the truth about a situation. Where is the Spirit pointing out our false ways of thinking, feeling, and acting? Where is the Spirit leading us into having a more accurate picture of reality? Where is the Spirit pointing out our destructive patterns of interacting with another and the rest of the world? Where is the Spirit creating something new in our midst? Where and how is the Spirit leading us into a more fruitful, more life-giving way of being together as a community? How can we distinguish what is false from what is true?

On the other hand, this list includes various capacities to do extraordinary things that a community might need: faith to believe that certain can happen (again, not to be confused with the faith all believers are given); the power to heal the sick; the capacity to perform miracles; and being able to speak in tongues and interpret tongues. All of these gifts have to do with power the Spirit gives certain people to do something extraordinary. The Spirit may, at certain points, endow some people in our communities with the capacity to receive and transmit a richer source of energy outside of themselves in order to accomplish a particular task. With God, all things are possible.

We are more familiar with Paul's second list: "And God has appointed in the church first apostles, second prophets, third teachers. . . ." (1 Cor. 12:28; see also Rom. 12:6-8). Apostles start new Christian communities by proclaiming the message of the cross. Prophets proclaim the gospel's truth and relate that truth to who we are becoming in Christ and what we are to do. Teachers interpret what has been handed down through the apostolic tradition and interpret it in light of our living experience of the Spirit. There are also the gifts of healing, miracles, and various kinds of tongues. Although there is nothing uniquely "Christian" about these extraordinary capacities—religious traditions throughout the world have had manifestations of healings and miracles—nonetheless, they are not excluded from the life of the church. "Signs and wonders" have been there from the beginning: in Jesus' own life and in the lives of early Christian congregations.

And, there are forms of assistance and forms of leadership. In the list in Romans, Paul added being compassionate to giving and leading. The church does not merely consist of those who preach and teach or perform extraordinary deeds. It also consists of those who care for others—especially the poor and disadvantaged—and those who lead by offering "wise counsel" at crucial junctures in the community's life (see Prov. 1:5; 11:14; 24:6).

How does the Spirit create unity among us as members of the body of Christ even as the Spirit intensifies the diversity among us, by energizing each of us with specific gifts or tasks to perform? First, through the Spirit's life within us, *we become more fully interdependent on one another.* This interdependence is different from either dependence or independence. We lose neither our dignity as individuals (by becoming dependent on others), nor our connection with them (by becoming wholly autonomous). Rather, and this is the paradox of life in the Spirit, we only truly benefit one another when we grow more fully into our differentiation from one another. This means that we need both fully to recognize how much others need our gifts and how much we need their gifts in order for all of us to function in a healthy way.

Can a foot say I do not belong to the body because I am not a hand? Can an ear say I do not belong to the body because I am not an eye? If the whole body were an eye, how would we be able to hear? If the whole body were an ear, how would we be able to smell? Just as the various members of the body need one another, so we who are members of Christ's body need one another. If we are to see, hear, and smell, we need eyes, ears, and noses. If we are to walk around, we need our feet (1 Cor. 12:14-26).

Second, through the Spirit's life within us, *we treat with greater respect those among us who are perceived to be less honorable or less respectable.* We cover our sexual organs in public in order to avoid shame. And yet, these organs are indispensable for the propagation of the species. By analogy, members of the body of Christ who appear to be weaker, needier, less honorable, and less respectable— members who by human standards would be considered "inferior" because of their poverty and their lack of social status—are, in fact, indispensable to the life of Christ's body.

God uses what is weak to shame the strong; God uses what is foolish to shame the wise. God uses "what is low and despised in the world, things that are not, to reduce to nothing things that are" (1 Cor. 1:26-28). God continually fills the hungry with good things, and sends the rich away empty. We empty the cross of its generative potency when we fail to attend to the needs of those who are weakest among us—a point relevant not only for our local communities, but for our understanding who we are as Christ's body throughout the world.

Third, through the Spirit's life within us, *we share in one another's joy and suffering.* Just as the whole human body suffers when one part of the body parts is in pain, so we who are members of Christ's body suffer with one another as we each suffer pain. Likewise, we rejoice with another as each one of us experiences life's successes and pleasures. The Spirit's life gives us the magnanimity and generosity of spirit to enter empathetically into other people's experiences without being threatened by them and without fearing that we will be engulfed by them. Unlike ancient or modern ideals of self-sufficiency, the body of Christ is about being fully empathetic with one another—being able to enter fully into one another's experiences and the full display of emotions those experiences entail, both positive and negative. We are in life together—with all the pleasures and pains that human lives in bodies undergo.

Discerning the "Body" of Christ

Conflicts within the Corinthian congregation became especially apparent in their celebration of the Lord's Supper. Like the community in Acts, they combined the ritual observance of Jesus' Last Supper with a community meal. When they would come together for these meals, some people would eat most of the food—and even get drunk—while others (probably the poorer members of the community, who had to come late because of work) would leave these meals hungry. Again, Paul reminded the community of the crucified Jesus in their midst: "As often as you eat the bread and drink the cup, you proclaim the Lord's death until he comes" (1 Cor. 11:26). Thus, we are to examine ourselves and only then come to the table. If we eat and drink without "discerning the body," we bring judgment on ourselves (1 Cor. 11:29).

What did he mean by this? To what did "the body" refer: Christ or the community? Through the Spirit, we all share in the body and blood of Christ. "Because there is one bread, we who are many are one body, for we all partake of the one bread" (1 Cor. 10:17). We are baptized into a corporate life with one another. When we fail to recognize one another's need, we violate the body of Christ we see in one another's faces.

But what does it mean to "discern the body"? How do we discern the body of Christ? How do we discern what the Spirit is doing in our midst? How do we distinguish what is true from what is false? How do we know when gifts are being used appropriately and when they are being used inappropriately? All the gifts listed in Paul's letter are human activities that non-Christians can enact as well. Other religious traditions have missionaries (apostles), prophets, teachers, leaders, and so on. The kinds of skills used in all of the gifts—teaching, preaching, caring for others—are human activities. Even the miraculous gifts of healing and speaking in tongues can be found in other traditions. How, then, do we distinguish truth from falsehood when we exercise these gifts?

We find two criteria for discerning the appropriate use of spiritual power in Paul's letter, criteria that resonate with those we found in the Johannine literature The first is the affirmation that "Jesus is Lord" (1 Cor. 12:3). Any inspiration that denies the proclamation of Jesus' death and resurrection and its saving import for all people has its source in something other than Christ's life-giving Spirit. This is not to say that the Spirit of God is not active throughout the world, giving us insight into God's creative work in the God in whom "we live and move and have our being" (Acts 17:28). God's Spirit permeates all of reality with truth. But the Christian community exists solely for one unique purpose: the proclamation of the gospel of Jesus Christ and its significance for all of humanity. Moreover, this criterion has within it an inherent judgment on all forms of power that would negate the kind of power enacted on our Lord's cross. Any activation of a gift that simply feeds infantile narcissism—and the envy and wrangling that goes along with it—will come under the Spirit's fire of judgment.

The second criterion follows directly from the first. The Spirit activates within us manifestations of the Spirit for the common good, for the upbuilding of the whole community. Special gifts often create difficulties. When a person has an extraordinary capacity to do something, it tends not only to create envy and jealousy in others, but it also tends to give that person an over-inflated sense of their importance—that everything in the community revolves around him or her. Further, it can create a sense of inferiority in others. And these difficulties are only magnified when they reach the level of conflict among factions within a community. Christian history is littered with factionalism, with competition among groups emerging around spiritual or theological leaders who have gained prominence through the power of their ideas or spiritual experiences and the force of their personalities. Additionally, often visible manifestations of supernatural phenomena have only led to further conflict. When a church has a spiritual revival or a charismatic renewal—for example, when some members start to speak in tongues or prophesy or perform miraculous healings—it often creates much division. Those who have these gifts think they are somehow more spiritually mature than others are; those who do not have these gifts are threatened by those who do.

Nonetheless, the Spirit energizes capacities within us not so that we can bring attention to ourselves, or make ourselves superior to or more "right" than others. We are not given gifts so that we can be paid more or gain more power and influence over others. Rather, we are given gifts so that we can build up the communities to which we belong (1 Cor. 14:4). We are given gifts to work for the common good, a good that benefits not only our interests but the interests of others as well. This means having a sober estimate of what we have to offer the communities of which we are a part—not thinking too highly of what we have to offer and not thinking too lowly of it either. Having a "sober estimate" means simply having an accurate picture of our distinctive contributions (Rom. 12:3).

Think of how different our communities would be if everyone not only fully entered into the full potency of their gifts, but also sought to use those gifts for building up the common good. Think of the strife we could avoid if we realized that we were given gifts not to secure our own interests—Christ has always taken care of that—but to contribute freely to the good of the whole. And when we think beyond the church, think of how different our cities, our nation, and even our world would be if gifted and talented individuals used all their capacities to help the least among us.

What would happen if the most talented teachers among us taught in schools in underprivileged neighborhoods? If the most talented doctors, dentists, and nurses worked in communities where health care was needed most? If the most talented carpenters and construction workers dedicated their lives to building homes for the homeless and those who could not afford to own homes? What would happen if our most gifted entrepreneurs used their capacity to make money to create jobs for people in parts of the world that were the most impoverished economically? What would happen if they chose to reinvest their profits and bonuses, rather than keep them for themselves, so that they could further invest in the communities they serve? What would happen if those with access to resources in wealthier nations used that wealth to create banks and credit agencies that could help start small businesses in poorer nations? The possibilities are endless, but with God, all things are possible!

The More Excellent Way

The climax of 1 Corinthians is the hymn of love in chapter 13. We often hear this hymn read at weddings and tend to associate it with romantic love and sentimental feelings. But there is nothing sentimental about the vision of love we find here. If anything, the hymn deals, in a very practical way, with the question of how we are to use our diverse gifts so that they build up the whole. As we exercise our particular gifts, we are to strive for the "greater gifts"—those that build up the church. Moreover, we are to strive for a "still more excellent way" (1 Cor. 12:31). What is that more excellent way? It is nothing other than the way of love (see Gal. 5:6).

We may strive for the highest of spiritual aspirations: speak in tongues; prophesy and understand all mysteries; have the faith to move mountains (and even give our bodies to be burned!). But without love, we are a noisy gong or a clanging cymbal; we are nothing; we gain nothing (1 Cor. 13:1-3). Love is patient, kind, not envious or boastful, or arrogant or rude. Love does not insist on its own way. Love is not irritable or resentful. Love does not rejoice in falsehood or wrongdoing, but rejoices in the truth. Love "bears all things, believes all things, hopes all things, endures all things" (13:4-7). And, unlike particular gifts, which are given for specific purposes, love never ends. Our gifts only give us a partial picture of the whole truth. But when the complete picture comes—when God's future is fully disclosed to us—all that is partial will come to an end (13:8-9).

With maturity comes the capacity not only to see how partial everything we do actually is, but also to appreciate how God's eternal and infinite creativity is so much greater than anything we could possible imagine (13:9-10).

In this life, "we walk by faith, not by sight" (2 Cor. 5:7). In the age to come, however, we will see God face to face. Now we only know in part, but then we will know fully, just as we have been fully known by God. We are first known and loved by God, and in God's knowing and loving us, we are able to know and love God, and know and love others (1 Cor. 13:12) What abides throughout is faith, hope, and love. *Faith* enables us to trust in what God has done for us through Christ. *Hope* gives us confidence that, indeed, God is working all things for good. But *love* is the greatest among these—God's everlasting love, which gives us the power and freedom not only to love God, but also to love ourselves and to love others with the same love (13:13).

For Reflection and Discussion

1. How does the message of the cross bring about reconciliation among people who are in competition with each other? How does the Spirit form us into the new humanity Christ's death and resurrection have ushered in?

2. How does the Spirit enable us to both grow more fully into the diverse gifts we have each been given individually, even as we grow more fully into unity with one another as members of Christ's body?

6

The Spirit Creates Hope

Life is difficult. M. Scott Peck begins *The Road Less Traveled* with this simple observation. Part of being human is facing the fact that life is not easy. We all face difficulties and afflictions—regardless of our personal circumstances, and regardless of our family, tribe, class, nation, race, or even species. Life is a series of problems. What may be most frustrating is that we often find that we do not always do the good that we want. Paul spoke for all of us when he said, "I do not do the good I want, but I do the very thing I hate" (Rom. 7:15). In our inmost selves, we want to love God above everything else and love others as we love ourselves. We want to be able to trust God in all things. We want to be good. We want to speak truth. We want do the right thing for ourselves and for those around us.

Yet instead, we find within us deeply embedded fears and psychic desires that seem to be in conflict with our best intuitions. In the face of these primal fears and desires, we find it difficult to trust God above all else. We find it difficult to love others and ourselves in freedom. Although we know the good we ought to do, we find ourselves divided. Our capacity to act is often stymied by the inability to do the good we want. We discover that what we do tends to be governed by reactions, more primal fears and desires, rather than the clarity of our best intuition. And, as we explore these reactions, we discover that we have, in fact, identified ourselves with, or defined ourselves by, something *other* than God—our status, our wealth, our health, our beauty, our relationships with people or institutions, what others think of us, and so on. We discover how we compulsively try to justify our existence by being right, being good, being valuable, being unique, being competent, having a lot of pleasure, having control over others—you fill in the blanks.

When we *fear* we will not get what we *desire*—what we have identified as something we *must* have for survival—we no longer can think or act clearly. We either become overly obsequious, handing over to others our rightful autonomy, or we become overly domineering and controlling, continually trying to figure out how we can use others to get what we want. We usually can see how these patterns are at work in other people's lives. It is more difficult to see these patterns at work in our own lives. How can we be liberated from all this? How does the gift of the Spirit, the gift of our adoption as children of God through Christ, make any difference in the way we actually live our lives?

The "Already" and the "Not Yet"

In his encounter with the risen Jesus, Paul experienced the power of the age beyond death. This experience radically changed his life. He felt compelled to tell the world a message about how a radically new relationship with God and with the rest of life was now possible. Something had happened, something new, which has the capacity to reverse what had previously seemed irreversible. The words of 2 Corinthians 5:17 express this best: "If anyone is in Christ, there is a new creation: everything old has passed away; see, everything has become new!"

Yet, Paul never allowed the tension between the *already* of this existing newness and the *not yet* of its fulfillment to slacken. He was still very conscious of the fact that in this life, on this side of death, we still live very much in the tension—the paradox—of being completely *free*, on the one hand, and of still being very much *bound* to the difficulties of this life, on the other. We are already justified (Rom. 5:1), yet we will await and hope for righteousness (Gal. 5:5). We are redeemed (Rom. 3:24), yet we still await the redemption of our bodies

(Rom. 8:23). Salvation has taken place in Christ's death and resurrection, yet we still await our full salvation (Rom. 5:9); we are still in the process of being saved (2 Cor. 2:15). We have "put on" Christ in baptism (Gal. 3:27), yet we are still urged to "put on the Lord Jesus Christ" as something not yet accomplished (Rom. 13:14).

Perhaps the most striking metaphor describing the already-not yet character of Christian faith is that of adoption. On the one hand, Paul stated, "For you did not receive a spirit of slavery to fall back into fear, but you *have received a spirit of adoption*" (Rom. 8:15, emphasis added). And yet, only a few verses later, he wrote, "And not only creation, but we ourselves, who have the first fruits of the Spirit, *groan inwardly while we wait for adoption*, the redemption of our bodies" (8:23, emphasis added). The experience of adoption always takes place in the paradox of the "here" and the "not yet." The renewing of our nature is only worked out in the dying that takes place in our mortal bodies and in our dying to all that is false, sinful, and unjust within us (see 2 Cor. 4:16–5:10). There is no other way to experience Christ but within our experience of this life, which is always also an experience of death, since mortal life is continually passing away.

How do we live in the midst of this paradox of the "here and not yet"? In the interval between the ages (between the old age of the forces of sin and death and the new age of Christ's Spirit), we have been given the "first fruits" of the Spirit, the first sheaf of the harvest that will come when the Spirit will, indeed, be poured out on all. We have been given a first installment of the full inheritance we are to receive (2 Cor. 1:22).

We have received the same Spirit that gave Jesus such intimacy with God, the same Spirit that enabled him to cry, "Abba! Father!" And when we do cry out to our "Abba," this very Spirit bears witness with our spirit that we are, indeed, children of God, and as children, heirs of all God has to offer (Rom. 8:15-17; Gal. 4:6). Through the Spirit's power within us, we *can* "set our minds" on the Spirit. We can perceive and respond to life from the vantage point of the Spirit's life within us. We can live according to the Spirit's life within us. Christ's life-giving Spirit, which is the very Spirit of God, has been poured into our lives, and through that Spirit we can, indeed, experience Christ within the totality of our lives (Rom. 8:9).

We now have the power to shift our attention away from destructive thoughts and feelings—from the destructive force fields of energy that permeate not only our individual psyches but also the communities and the world we are a part of—and focus instead on the good the Spirit's force field of energy is creating in our midst (Rom. 8:5-7). From the vantage point of the Spirit's life within us, we need no longer be so preoccupied with our fears and desires but can instead step into the fullness of what life has to offer. We can mature into the gifts and talents we have been given so that we can be a source of life for others—in our families, in our work, and in our communities. We can see that, in spite of our difficulties, God has a purpose for us.

Nonetheless, all the Spirit's power within us is only experienced in our finite, fragile bodies. There is no way around the fact that we will die eventually and that every day we undergo the deaths of our frustrated desires and expectations. There is no way around our struggle with sin and the fact that all that is false within us must be put to death. We have no choice about this: die we will, like it or not. And yet, with the Spirit, there is a difference. The same Spirit who raised Jesus from the dead now dwells within us and gives life to our mortal bodies (Rom. 8:11). Even though our bodies are fragile and dying, we can experience the Spirit's power as the power of life beyond death. Indeed, it is precisely in the "clay jars" of our mortal experience that the "extraordinary power" of God is made manifest in our lives. "We have this treasure in clay jars, so that it may be made clear that this extraordinary power belongs to God and does not come from us" (2 Cor. 4:7).

While we live, we are being given up to death for Jesus' sake so that the life of Jesus might be made visible in our mortal flesh. Our daily dying, our daily suffering, is no longer merely an exercise in futility. Rather it is precisely the place where we carry in our bodies the death of Jesus, so that the life of Jesus may be visible in those very bodies (2 Cor. 4:10). Death is at work in our lives so that life can be at work in the lives of others: "death is at work in us, but life in you" (2 Cor. 4:12). The Spirit bears witness to the full inheritance we have through Christ, precisely as we "suffer with him so that we may also be glorified with him" (Rom. 8:17).

With the Spirit's power, we allow all that is false within us to die, and we find that we are able to shift out of our reactive patterns and enter into a more generative and creative way of being in the world. With the Spirit's power, we allow Christ to heal and forgive all that is sinful and diseased within us, and we are able to shift out of our self-preoccupation. We can shift out of our preoccupation with securing our interests in the face of our primal fears and desire, so that we can, in fact, attend to the good that needs to be done, both for others and for ourselves. We can speak the truth that needs to be heard. We can do the good that needs to be done. We can live our lives with grace and beauty.

But there is no way around the paradox that all this extraordinary power only takes place within the suffering and weakness of our mortal bodies. We will not escape any of life's difficulties. Paul's difficulties included, among others, "afflictions, hardships, calamities, beatings, imprisonments, riots, labors, sleepless nights, hunger" (2 Cor. 6:4-5). Ours may not be as dramatic as his were, but they are real nonetheless. Yet, in the midst of our difficulties, we can still affirm, with Paul, that something more powerful is at work in and through them: "We are afflicted in every way, but not crushed; perplexed, but not driven to despair; persecuted, but not forsaken; struck down, but not destroyed" (2 Cor. 4:8-9). And, "We are treated as impostors, and yet are true; as unknown, and yet are well known; as dying, and see—we are alive; as punished, and yet not killed; as sorrowful, yet always rejoicing; as poor, yet making many rich; as having nothing, and yet possessing everything" (2 Cor. 6:8-10).

Marrtin Luther did something that was truly revolutionary when he transferred the concept of vocation (*vocatio*) to people's daily lives. It is precisely in our daily lives—at home, at work, in the society at large—that the Spirit works, enacting the kingdom of God. It is there, in the natural communities and personal relationships that make up our lives, that we experience the paradox of the new age of the Spirit being ushered in even amidst the suffering and work of life. It is there, in the particular details of our lives, that the Spirit endows us with the power to participate in God's purposes being enacted in our midst. It is there in these particular details that our inner nature is renewed and conformed to Christ's image within. It is there that we are empowered to shift the focus off our desires and fears so that we can attend to the good that needs to be done for those around us.

I think of my father caring for my mother with Alzheimer's. His grief and mourning over the loss of his wife is palpable. His anger with God over why God allows such things is real. Nonetheless, in the midst of his grief and his anger, there is also a very real sense not only of joy but also of what can only be described as "extraordinary power"—a youthfulness, a buoyancy, and a lightness of being, a delight in life, and a profound sense of agency.

I think of an interview I heard on the radio, where former Minnesota governor Al Quie described the most difficult political decision he had made in his life—the decision not to run again so that he could make the hard choices and difficult compromises that would need to be made if he was to attend to Minnesota's economic difficulties adequately. Even his Democratic opponent, Roger Moe, who was also being interviewed on the same show, observed that the next governor of the state would not have had such economic success had Quie not made the tough decisions that needed to be made during his tenure as governor.

I think of Nalini Arles, an Indian theologian who recently was a visiting professor at my seminary. A Dalit (considered "untouchable" within the caste system in India), she has committed her life to empowering her people so that they can realize their full stature as those created in God's image, in spite of the ways they have been stigmatized by the caste system. Although she has a very busy schedule as a seminary professor, she and her husband have managed to find the time to organize a foundation committed to providing education for Dalit youth and advocating on behalf of their rights and needs.

The Spirit in the Groaning of Creation

We are not the only ones who live with the paradox of extraordinary power within suffering and weakness. We are not the only ones who groan as our nature is being renewed (2 Cor. 4:16). The inner renewal that takes place in our personal lives is also taking place in the cosmos as a whole. Our personal rebirth anticipates the rebirth of the entire cosmos. Precisely as we become more aware of the possibility of life in God's truth and God's justice, we become more aware that we are not the only ones who experience the futility of life in this passing of age. Others experience it as well. Not only we, but also all of creation longs to have its spoilt and neglected possibilities given back. All of creation longs for the vitalizing energy of God's Spirit.

As the Spirit works in our lives, we become more aware of the suffering of others and their yearning for a time when truth and justice will prevail. We become more aware of how the weak throughout the world yearn to be freed from their powerful oppressors. We will become more aware of how others yearn for a time when God will wipe away all tears, and death will be no more, for a time when God will be with God's people, and God with them will be their God, saying, "See, I am making all things new" (Rev. 21:3-5).

In the same way that Israel cried out to be liberated from slavery in Egypt, we too cry out for the liberation of the whole cosmos. We too cry out with the rest of creation for a time when God will heal the hurts of all people. We too cry out for a time when all forms of exploitation and injustice will cease. We too cry out for the vision of the new creation the prophets anticipated. We too cry out to live in harmony with the natural world. We too cry out for a time when the vitalizing energy of the Spirit will prove to be more powerful than any destructive force or pattern, not only within us, but also within our communities and society, and indeed in all of creation!

Our cries are not futile; they are buoyed by hope. We have received the "first fruits" of the Spirit and we can live in hope. This is not a hope that things will always go our way. This hope does not give us control over all that happens in our lives. Even Jesus did not fulfill his followers' hope that he would liberate them from their Roman oppressors. Rather, this hope is for something that is both much deeper and much more expansive. It is a fundamental confidence that God's purposes for the world are benevolent—that God is working all things "together for good" in every situation we or others may have to face (Rom. 8:28). This hope helps us see that the forces of good in the world are far more powerful than the force of evil, and it gives us the power to work with others in using all the capacities and talents the Spirit gives us to create just and merciful communities and societies. This hope gives us the power to work with others in caring for God's good creation

The metaphor of childbearing describes how the Spirit gives birth to this hope both as it emerges within all of creation and in our lives as well. Like a mother giving birth to a child, our groaning is precisely the place where God is creating new possibilities for life, both within us and in the world around us. In whatever difficulty others or we may be facing, in whatever suffering others or we may endure, God is creating new possibilities. Our suffering, therefore, is always a *creative suffering*. We are not merely powerless in the face of destructive forces within ourselves or within our communities and societies. As God's children, we can act in ways that correspond to

God's reign in the world. We can work with others for righteousness and justice. We can speak the truth in love. We can do the good that needs to be done in our midst. We can do the right thing we have been called to do. We can use all our gifts and capacities and work with others for the common good. Through the Spirit's power, we can give birth to Christ's life within us as that life takes a concrete form within the particular details of our lives.

Prayer in the Spirit

As we groan, giving birth to Christ's life within us, we may not even know how to pray. Nonetheless, it is precisely there, in our inarticulate—often confused and sometimes despairing—groans, that the Spirit intercedes for us "with sighs too deep for words" (Rom. 8:26). In our deepest moments of despair or joy, and even in those times when we are rendered speechless (either by life's pain or life's pleasurable delight), the Spirit buttresses our prayers. In the midst of our weakness, the Spirit is there, giving us confidence in God's extraordinary power to heal, to forgive, to transform, and to bring about wholeness and completion in every moment we experience.

For centuries, mystics have understood that in our prayers, the Spirit prays through us. Prayer is actually about entering into a conversation within God. We are not alone in our prayers, but the Spirit intercedes through us. And God, who for Paul was always the one Jesus called "Abba," not only searches our hearts in our prayers, but knows the mind of the Spirit. As the Spirit searches the very depths of God, giving us access to those depths, God also knows what is on the Spirit's mind, what the Spirit's intentions are for us (Rom. 8:27). And the Spirit's intentions through our prayers are precisely to transform our deepest desires into yearnings for God's truth and God's justice. The Spirit seeks to conform us to Christ's image, so that we can truly be "sons" and "daughters" of God—sons and daughters who do God's will in the world. This is why prayer is so powerful. Not only is prayer buoyed by the Spirit's intercession for us, but also in the very process of prayer our deepest desires are transformed into yearnings for God's purposes for us and the world around us.

What happens in prayer? As we, like Jesus, cry out to his Abba with our paradoxical prayers—"take this cup from me" yet "not my will, but yours"—the Spirit does indeed transform our deepest desires into yearnings for God's truth and God's justice. The Spirit helps us see that, indeed, all things work together for good. God's benevolent purposes are at work in the universe, in spite of evidence that seems to contradict them (Rom. 8:28). The Spirit gives us the faith to live more fully into Christ's life within us. The Spirit gives us hope to enter more fully into God's loving intentions for us. We begin to see that in both life and death—in both pleasure and pain, in both good and bad—God is at work forgiving, healing, and bringing about something new.

Through the Spirit we can see that our lives are located in the infinite creativity of God's eternal life. We can see that God's inexhaustible and creative life precedes and follows all that happens to us. God not only knows us in all eternity but also wills in all eternity that we share in the intimacy God has with Jesus, the intimacy a loving parent has with a beloved child. We can see that God's intentions are nothing other than to conform us to the image of Christ, so that we can be part of God's large family. By faith in Jesus, we too are chosen and called; by faith in Jesus we too are placed in a right relationship with God and given all the splendor and wonder that belongs to a chosen child (Rom. 8:29-30).

The Spirit Imbues Us with God's Love through Jesus

What then are we to say about all of this? If God is for us, then who can be against us? God did not withhold what was dearest to God, God's own chosen child, but gave him up to benefit all of us (Rom. 8:31-32). We can be sure that after such a gift God will not refuse anything God can give.

Who can accuse us? What can cause us to feel shame or guilt? What can cause us to despair? Can anyone accuse those whom God has chosen? When God acquits, who can condemn? Jesus, the one who died and rose again, is, along with the Spirit, within God interceding for us. Our lives are lived within their Trinitarian prayer. What can separate us from God's love for us in Jesus? Can the difficulties we now experience separate us from this love? Can the troubles and worries of life separate us from God's love? Can the lack of food or clothes separate us from God's love? Can being threatened and attacked separate us from God's love? Can natural disaster, war, and persecution separate us from this love? (Rom. 8:34-35)

Of course, God's promise does not make us immune to life's difficulties. But it does give us the boldness to cry out, as the people of Israel did in their times of greatest affliction: "Because of you we are being killed all day long, and accounted as sheep for the slaughter. Rouse yourself! Why do you sleep, O Lord? Awake, do not cast us off forever!" (Ps. 44:22-23). Confident in God's love for us, we can have the courage to face whatever it is that we are facing, confident that whether we live or die, we are in God's hands. We need not fear life, but can enter fully into all the possibilities God has in store for us. We need not fear death, not just our final death, but also the daily deaths we experience as our expectations and desires are frustrated by the realities of life. In either life or death, we know by faith that we are embraced by God's inexhaustible life and love. We need not fear any other powers in the world. We need not fear angels or demons, or any other form of spiritual power. We need not fear the powers of nature, or the disasters they can bring down in the form of earthquakes or floods (Rom. 8:38-39).

And, perhaps more significantly, we need not fear any other human beings, regardless of how threatening they may be to us. The Spirit's life within us gives us the capacity to stand up to every narcissistic or tyrannical power who would seek to control us, who takes up the space that would enable us to think, feel, and act freely.

This is why talk about the Spirit "being poured out on all flesh" is so threatening to anyone who seeks to control others—whether they are the demons of the Gospel stories or the difficult human beings we have to deal with in our own lives. Through the Spirit, we can fully enter into the dignity of our humanity, confident that God's love will never forsake us.

We need not fear anything in time. We need not fear the past, nor the resentments, shame, guilt, or regret that may plague our memories. Nothing we have done or that anyone else has done to us can separate us from God's love. Although the past is irreversible, from the standpoint of God's creative life, we continue to stand in the fresh new vitality that God's life sustains.

We need not fear the future, for nothing that could possibly happen to us in the future can separate us from God's creative love. Although the future is unpredictable, we need not fear its vagaries because whatever may come of us, we will continually find ourselves in God's loving embrace. We need not fear the present, with its very real limits and possibilities, since in every moment we stand within the promise of God's creative and loving power. We need not fear anything in space. In Luther's words, "Nothing is so small but God is still smaller, nothing so large but God is still larger, nothing is so short but God is still shorter, nothing so long but God is still longer, nothing is so broad but God is still broader, nothing so narrow but God is still narrower."[1] In the psalmist's words, God hems us in, behind, and before us. If we ascend to heaven, God is there. If we descend to death and hell, Jesus has been there too (Ps. 139). We need not fear constriction and restraints. We need not fear expansion and permeable boundaries. God's infinite and creative life permeates all things. Regardless of what happens to us, our feet are set in the "broad place" where there is no cramping (Ps. 31:8), the spacious and expansive roominess of God's eternal and creative life.

For this reason, we can continually kneel in prayer before God, the loving parent of the chosen child, Jesus, the one in whom family in heaven and on earth takes its name. With confidence, we can pray that, from the abundant resources in divine life, God will strengthen our innermost selves with power through Christ's Spirit. We can pray that Christ may dwell in our hearts through faith, as we are being rooted and grounded in his love. We can pray that we may have the power to comprehend, with all the saints, the full scope of this love—its breadth, height, length, and depth. We can pray that we know the fullness of Christ's love, which surpasses all knowledge, so that we may be filled with the fullness, the very plenitude of God's life. All is ours, not just the past, the present, and the future, but also the dimensions of space—and even all human, natural, and supernatural powers—indeed, life and death itself!

Through the Spirit's power, we can live by faith in Christ's life within us, a faith that is only "worked out" in love for others and ourselves. Regardless of what we face, whether it is good or bad, or pleasurable or painful, the Spirit is at work in us, giving us the hope to see that God's love is at the heart of reality—not only for us, but also for all people and all of creation itself.

For Reflection and Discussion

1. How do we experience the "already" and "not yet" character of the Spirit's presence in our lives? How is the extraordinary power of the Spirit experienced within the difficulties we face in life?

2. How does the Spirit give us hope even as we, and the rest of creation, are painfully aware of the suffering and evil that still exists in this world?

3. Why can we still affirm that God "works all things for good" when life often appears to contradict this? Related to this, how does the Spirit transform our deepest desires into yearnings for God's purposes in the world?

Notes

Chapter Two

1. Jürgen Moltmann, *The Way of Jesus Christ,* trans. Margaret Kohl (Minneapolis: Fortress Press, 1995), 108.

Chapter Three

1. Jürgen Moltmann, *The Church in the Power of the Spirit*, trans. Margaret Kohl (Minneapolis: Fortress Press, 1993), 40.

Chapter Six

1. Martin Luther, *Luther's Works*, vol. 37 (Philadelphia: Fortress Press, 1961), 228.

For Further Reading

Dunn, James. *Jesus and the Spirit: A Study of the Religious and Charismatic Experience of Jesus and the First Christians as Reflected in the New Testament.* Grand Rapids, Mich.: Eerdmans, 1997.

This book explores the religious experiences of early Christians, starting first with Jesus' experience of the Spirit and of being God's Son and moving on to the experiences of the Spirit described in Acts and in Paul's letters.

Kim, Kirsteen. *The Holy Spirit in the World: A Global Conversation.* Maryknoll, N.Y.: Orbis, 2007.

This book sets a theology of the Holy Spirit within a global context, drawing both on Scripture and on a range of theologies of the Spirit that are emerging from throughout the world.

Moltmann, Jürgen. *Spirit of Life: A Universal Affirmation.* Minneapolis: Augsburg, 1992.

This book is probably the best contemporary theology of the Spirit. Drawing on the Bible and on classical and contemporary theology, this book speaks in very vivid ways about how the Spirit gives life not only to us as individuals, but to our communities and societies, and the natural world.

Montague, George. *The Holy Spirit: Growth of a Biblical Tradition.* Eugene, Ore.: Wipf & Stock, 2006.

This book is one of the most thorough studies of the Holy Spirit in the Bible, offering careful exegesis of how different books in the Bible depict the work of the Holy Spirit.

Prenter, Regin. *Spiritus Creator*. Eugene, Ore.: Wipf and Stock, 2001.
   This book is the best study available of Martin Luther's theology of the Holy Spirit, drawing on both his early and later writings.